COLEMAN HAWKINS

COLEMAN HAWKINS

Burnett James

Selected discography
by Tony Middleton

Spellmount
TUNBRIDGE WELLS

Hippocrene Books
NEW YORK

First published in the UK in 1984 by
SPELLMOUNT LTD
12 Dene Way, Speldhurst,
Tunbridge Wells, Kent TN3 0NX
ISBN 0 946771 11 1 (UK)

James, Burnett
    Coleman Hawkins. – (Jazz masters)
    1. Hawkins, Coleman 2. Jazz musicians –
    United States – Biography
    I. Title II. Series
785.42'092'4 ML419.H/

First published in the USA by
HIPPOCRENE BOOKS INC.
171 Madison Avenue,
New York, NY 10016

ISBN 0 87052 009 1 (USA)

Series editor: John Latimer Smith
Cover design: Peter Theodosiou

Printed & bound in Great Britain
by Anchor/Brendon Ltd, Tiptree, Essex

Contents

Beginnings and Ends

If, as the late Roland Kirk put it, jazz is 'black classical music', some interesting consequences follow. For one thing, it requires not only classic performances but also classic performers; performances, that is, which stand the test of time (and not simply the test of passing fashion), and performers who make a genuine advance in both style and technique. Without such figures and such performances, no art form can develop and therefore no classic art can emerge.

In jazz there are a few records that perpetuate unquestioned classic performances. One is Louis Armstrong's *West End Blues*; another is Coleman Hawkins's 1939 *Body and Soul*. There are others, but rather less than may at first be suspected. The classic artist is a rare phenomenon; the artist who both creates the conditions for the emergence of the classic and then proceeds to produce it himself (or herself) is rarer still. Armstrong, Hawkins, Charlie Parker certainly come into this category, Sidney Bechet and Lester Young probably, and of course Duke Ellington although in a slightly different sense and context.

Coleman Hawkins did not of course invent the saxophone in jazz. he did not even 'invent' the tenor saxophone. There were other saxophonists around during his youth – each making a contribution, as he himself admitted freely, and even asserted against exaggerated claims made on his own behalf – semi-legendary figures like Stump Evans, Happy Cauldwell, Prince Robinson. But he also agreed when pressed that he did evolve a genuinely new style and was already playing in a manner quite different from the others. Exactly what that manner was and how it emerged and matured must be the primary task that any study of him has to undertake. He and his work became classics of jazz, his influence stronger and more widespread than any but Louis Armstrong's, at least until the coming of Charlie Parker. As the late Paul Gonsalves, for twenty years Duke Ellington's featured tenor, once said, as quoted by Stanley Dance in *The World of Duke Ellington* –

'Coleman Hawkins was my main influence. There was something in his music that coincided with Duke's that for me denoted class. Apart from his musicianship, there was something about him personally – the way he held his horn, the way he dressed. I called him "the Duke Ellington of the saxophone". His style seemed more musical than that of other tenors, a kind of classic way of playing. I admired Lester Young, but Coleman Hawkins was *it* for me.'

9

Young Hawk

The story of Coleman Hawkins is almost exclusively the story of the music he made and the bands he played with. Unlike some others, he did not sing (except very occasionally), or dance, or do handstands either on the stage or off it. He dedicated his entire life to playing the tenor saxophone, and in the end he played it as well as it could be played. He did virtually nothing else over the whole of his sixty-four and a half years of life.

He was born on 21 November 1904, in St Joseph, Missouri, into a reasonably well-to-do family. It was a large family too, but no other member appears to have taken seriously to music as a career. Unlike some other jazzmen of later repute, Coleman Hawkins was not brought up in poverty and deprivation. Nor was the Hawkins family in the affluent class of that period; all the same its means were sufficient to afford him a decent education and a social upbringing that, especially in his early years, gave him a personal confidence and a certain sophistication, at least in his first engagements in the unruly scramble of the music business.

He attended Junior School in St Joseph and in Kansas City, and then studied music first at Washburn College, Topeka, and then in Chicago. It seems to have been his mother who was determined that he should take up a musical career. It was she who gave him his first saxophone, on his ninth birthday, after he had been learning, first the piano and then the cello since he was five. Everything points to the emergence of a species of child prodigy. He may not have appeared before the public in short pants and ruffles, but he certainly mastered various aspects of music from an early age. From the outset he had that absolute dedication to what he was doing which is one of the hallmarks of genius and of what is now called star quality.

As soon as he laid hands on the tenor saxophone, he knew it was his instrument, above all other instruments. He mastered, in due course, both the clarinet and the bass saxophone, and probably the baritone as well, if contemporary photographs are to be taken as evidence; but it was the tenor which claimed his primary attention. From the beginning he spent all his time practising, apparently impervious to the claims of more childish and time-consuming demands. This was to be the pattern throughout his youth and young manhood at least.

There is not a great deal of information available about Hawkins's early working life. He certainly gigged with school bands while still a kid in short pants (probably), and he seems to have begun playing professionally – i.e. getting paid for it – from about the age of fifteen. In 1918 it is recorded that he left home and made for New York, after playing with various local groups in the Kansas City district. While studying music in Chicago, he had already heard some of the great jazzmen, including King Oliver, the young Louis Armstrong, Earl Hines and a number of others. it was then that the jazz idiom began to sink deep into him and claim his allegiance. He was gaining experience all the time, but so far there was little indication of the trail blazing, pathfinding virutoso soon to come. There is a little recorded evidence of the way he was playing before he officially joined Fletcher Henderson in 1924, but virtually nothing to suggest the evolutions, almost the wrath so far as saxophone players were concerned, that was in the making.

Details of these years are meagre and often contradictory. Whether or not it took place in Missouri or in New York, or during some intermission between the two, it is recorded history that he joined blues singer Maimie Smith's Jazz Hounds in the summer of 1921. This was his first significant professional engagement. Hitherto he had played with local bands, and with a few more in New York; now he was with a real 'name' band, on tour, and in a position to gain his first countrywide exposure. The Jazz Hounds was indeed an important group; and among its prominent members were the great trumpeter Bubber Miley, soon to make such an unforgettable mark with the emergent Duke Ellington orchestra, and the versatile reed man Garvin Bushell.

Coleman Hawkins was not yet a remarkable or a true stylist in the music he made, but he was certainly musically literate. In later years his favourite pastimes were said to be cooking beans and listening to string quartets. His culinary predilections were responsible for the nickname 'Bean' which he acquired and which frequently appears on record sleeves and album titles and in the titles of tunes written by, for, or about him. His propensity for attending concerts of the classics was something that prevailed through most of his life, and this was clearly another aspect of his musical literacy. Unlike some other famous jazzmen, too, he was always a good sight reader, able to find his way around the most complex arrangements, and that was to stand him well when he played with the Fletcher Henderson orchestra and encountered there scores that were by no means simple and straightforward, and some of which tended to floor less schooled musicians.

11

Although details are scanty, it is clear that Hawkins toured widely with Maimie Smith until well into 1923, gaining confidence and experience all the time. Not that he ever lacked confidence, especially personal confidence, but he was still only a teenager. His first commercial recording is usually taken to be the Okeh Maimie Smith number, *I'm gonna get you*, cut in late 1922. He certainly appeared on other recordings around the same time, and probably with various groups, but it seems unlikely that these contain anything memorable enough from Hawkins to ensure their revival, let alone immortality. The interest remains academic.

He appears, however and even this early in his career, to have been regarded with some awe, not to say trepidation, by other saxophone players and he was always ready to take part in 'cutting contests', invariably coming out on top, as was his custom for virtually the whole of his working life. But even that only signifies so far: the state of jazz saxophone playing in the early 1920s was not such as to ensure immortality for anyone who triumphed in these contests. It was one thing for a trumpet player, a trombonist, a clarinetist, even a pianist, to win fame by cutting his rivals, but for a rising star of the saxophone the competition, though by no means incompetent, was too far outside the mainstream of jazz to count for the same.

Although the saxophone was soon to become uniquely associated in the popular mind with the jazz idiom, indeed to some extent to become synonymous with it, the instrument itself was accepted only with some reluctance in the first outbreak of jazz and with even deeper reluctance into the classic New Orleans line-up, where it had virtually no established place at all. The saxophone as the jazz instrument *par excellence*, really arrived with the big bands, where there was particular scope not only for brilliant soloists but where a fully formed reed section played a role somewhat similar to that of the string section in a symphony orchestra.

Later, of course, when the saxophone was established and had in fact become a major jazz voice – though it was never the unique one – its use and application expanded and it became a prominent voice in small groups, frequently the one solo voice in what is sometimes referred to, not quite accurately, as jazz chamber music. Apart from a few outstanding altoists – like Hodges, Carter and later Charlie Parker – the main solo saxophone voice was to become the tenor, and that it did so was entirely due to the pioneering work of Coleman Hawkins. Even the later evolutions, as instigated by Lester Young principally, were made possible by what Hawkins had done. Just as Dizzy Gillespie once offered Louis Armstrong thanks 'for giving me my livelihood', so every saxophone player, certainly every tenor saxophonist, to whatever 'school' he or she may belong, should give thanks and pay homage to Coleman Hawkins. Miles Davis is reported once to have admonished a young tenor player of the 'cool' persuasion who was sneering at Hawkins, by reminding him that, if it had not been for Hawk, he would not be playing at all.

Inevitably, it did not all come together at once. There are some artists whose personal style seems to have been born with them, who, like Minerva, sprang fully armed from the sea. Johnny Hodges seems to have been one of these, figuratively speaking at least. But for Coleman Hawkins it was not so. It took a number of years and much determined effort for him to release the tenor saxophone from the limitations of the period and its stylistic solecisms. There was still much in his early work of the vulgar, of the coarseness of tone, and the slap-tonguing with which contemporary saxophone players sought to make their somewhat nebulous impression. For a man like Coleman Hawkins, determined as he was to evolve a personal style that would at the same time become a valid universal style, the main problem was twofold; to liberate the tenor saxophone from its all too familiar and more or less ubiquitous antics from which it derived its bad reputation, and at the same time to give it a distinctive voice which would finally establish it as an important and properly relevant voice in instrumental jazz. That he succeeded as magisterially as he did is perhaps tribute enough to the quality of his determination and the force of his genius.

In the meantime he continued to gig around in New York, to record when opportunity offered, to tour with Maimie Smith when required to do so, and generally to extend and consolidate his growing reputation.

He played for a while with Wilbur Sweatman's band, the group with which the very young Duke Ellington first featured as a pianist, around 1920. Otherwise Hawk seems to have worked in various New York clubs when not touring with Maimie Smith and the Jazz Hounds. But precisely what he did and where he did it is perhaps less important than some people of a determinedly documentary or analytical turn of mind may like to insist. During these years Hawkins was not so much finding his feet as working out how best to balance upon them; how, musically, he could best lay firm foundations for what was to come; and at the same time expanding his working experience, and establishing himself where it mattered.

The next major step in his artistic evolution was waiting, only a year or two in the future.

Deep Henderson

There is some confusion about the time when Coleman Hawkins joined the Fletcher Henderson orchestra. The year usually given for his becoming officially a member is 1924. Yet there is a famous photograph of the 1922 Henderson band in which Hawkins appears next to Don Redman, both of them festooned with all manner of saxophones and clarinets. Also, there are record dates under Henderson's name before 1924 on which Hawkins appears. It is sometimes argued that Hawkins sat in with the Henderson bands for recording or other purposes before becoming a regular member. This may be so; but it still does not explain a number of peculiarities, notably the 1922 picture which shows him definitely *in situ* and looking as though he both belonged there and knew it.

There is little doubt that, according to the custom of the times, Hawkins did occupy various chairs for specific purposes and was probably not a regular member of any group, not even the Jazz Hounds when Maimie was not on tour. He was still a young blood making his way in a musical environment full of good opportunities which could be exploited several ways by a sharp-witted and enterprising young man on the musical make. It is not all that important in the context of Hawkins's life and career as a whole. All it may mean is that he spent a dozen years with Henderson rather than the ten usually specified in the record books.

Whichever year first saw him a regular Henderson sideman, it was with Fletcher Henderson during the years up to 1934 that he established himself as the supreme master of the tenor saxophone and one of the greatest of all jazz soloists. He entered the Henderson ranks as an accomplished and literate musician but as a still embryonic stylist. By the time he left, the entire jazz world honoured him as one of its formative figures, a mature master who had no peer on his chosen instrument and very few on any other, indeed as one of the most influential musicians of his time.

Yet it still took time. His early work with Henderson was seldom remarkable. Except for a certain poise and naturally exuberant self-confidence, his solo work on the tenor saxophone did not register as anything out of the ordinary. He was soon to change all that, but to begin with there was more groundwork to be done and progress to be made. Partly no doubt this was linked to the musical setting. Until he joined

Henderson, Hawkins had worked in various different contexts, but apart from Maimie Smith's band he had no settled musical 'home'. And it does seem likely that, especially in view of the pioneering he was called upon to do, he needed a settled and permanent musical setting and background from which to develop his particular skills. Permanent membership of the Henderson band gave him this. Over the ten or twelve years during which Hawk was in the Henderson ranks, the band became one of the finest and most famous in the US, at its peak rivalling all others and outshining most. Even the Ellington band could not 'cut' it on the stands; indeed, many of Duke's own men declared that Henderson's was the best band in the business around 1930 and was the only one they felt trepidation in facing when it came to an outright contest. With scores by Don Redman and Henderson himself principally, and soloists of the calibre of Jimmy Harrison (tb), Joe Smith (t), Buster Bailey (cl) and several others of outstanding quality as well as the fast maturing Hawk himself, this was a band to be both respected and feared.

Like Hawkins himself, the Henderson band took a while to get into its full stride. But there is nothing singular in that: most bands, including Ellington's, needed time to find their feet, get the feel of the ground, for the individual members to coalesce into a group instead of being a collection of individual talents. But once in full cry, only poor management or economic stringency could prevent the Henderson band from reaching the top and staying there. Sadly, both the quality of its management and the economic pressures of the Depression years worked to undermine the band's authority and well-being. Fortunately, this did not operate seriously during Hawkins's years.

To begin with, as part of a two- or three-man reed section, Hawkins played bass saxophone and clarinet in solo and supporting roles in addition to his work on tenor. He is heard on clarinet on several tracks, and indeed he continued to be occasionally featured on it in various contexts during the following years. He is also heard in a number of instances on bass saxophone, that grunting and footpadding creation of Adolphe Sax which, during the 1920s in particular, was quite popular in jazz bands. Its leading exponent was Adrian Rollini, who used it not only for laying down bass foundations but also exploited it with some agility as a melody instrument. Others, like Min Liebrook, heard on a number of Bix Beiderbecke recordings, followed Rollini's example with some skill, and many others did so with greater or lesser success. Nor was it the white disciples of Rollini who appear in the record listings: Otto Hardwick sometimes played bass sax with the early Duke Ellington band, though not always with sure fingers or accurate tuning. Hawkins apparently turned his hand to baritone as well as bass (unless he kept the baritone handy to store his lunch in) for it appears in the 1922 photograph.

Hawkins did not become a notable viruoso on the bass saxophone, and it is unlikely that he ever aspired to. In any case, the bass saxophone fairly soon went out of fashion and was dropped from most bands. There are still a few loyal adherents around, like Harry Gold, who retain a strange but genuine, though probably Freudian, affection for the dinosaur of the saxophone family, so that it cannot be said to be extinct. Hawkins continued to play it occasionally in the Henderson band for some years, taking a few solos dotted around the scores, as in the 1928 *Old Black Joe Blues*, and filling in the textures where required. His clarinet work was rather more frequent.

The familiar style of the early saxophone players was largely staccato, rhythmically turgid, and harmonically unadventurous. In his early work, and even after he had taken his seat in the Henderson band, Coleman Hawkins played largely in this style but did it rather better than anyone else and a great deal better than most. Exactly when he came to the realization that to create a style on the tenor saxophone that would place it on a equal footing with trumpet, trombone and clarinet (as the classic jazz instrumental lineup) he would need to discover and develop the instrument's legato possibilities, is not precisely known. But it is certain that an event which took place in October 1924 had a major influence. This was the arrival in the trumpet section of a young recruit, formerly with King Oliver's Creole Jazz Band, his name Daniel Louis Armstrong.

There could hardly have been a greater contrast than between Coleman Hawkins and Louis Armstrong at that time. Louis, though already a brilliant instinctive musician of undoubted genius but in person a social hick, was at the opposite pole to the already sophisticated and dapper Hawk, lettered in both music and social matters but with his genius as yet unlocked. The conjunction or juxtaposition of the two was symptomatic of both the general situation of jazz during those years and of Fletcher Henderson's relationship with it. Henderson himself was the son of well-to-do professional people who, like most of their kind, did not think of music, and least of all jazz, as a suitable profession for their offspring. He seems in fact to have drifted into music more or less by accident when, coming to New York to continue his formal education, he found money short and supplemented it by random work for a music publishing company. He found the work congenial and so drifted into a permanent way of life in the music business. It was undoubtedly Henderson's background of respectability and his easy-going, unargumentative nature which made him acceptable as a Negro in the contemporary musical environment which was dominated by whites. It did not save him from the current race prejudice, or later secure him profitable employment in places where the lucrative jobs went to white musicians; but it did make life easier for him at a time when segregation in the music business was even more harsh than it was later or, in a number of respects, is now.

Henderson's was a sophisticated band, his men mostly of some personal standing. Coleman Hawkins certainly came into that category. Louis Armstrong, on the other hand, was a gauche young puppy whose ideas on dress and general deportment were the reason and cause for making him the butt of his colleagues in the band. His one unmistakable and unimpeachable bonus was his musical genius, and as soon as that was demonstrated and recognized within the band, respect for him was assured.

For one thing, Louis was a poor reader, and that in a band which relied much on written arrangements, was not helpful. There is a story that during one rehearsal Louis was diligently trying to play his part, but was reprimanded for playing at full blast all through. He retorted that he was playing what was written; but when it was pointed out to him that his part was in places marked *pp*, he said that he assumed that meant 'pound plenty'. It was an original interpretation, but it hardly endeared him to colleagues who knew their business. Coleman Hawkins was said to have remained more or less silent all through these altercations, which he regarded with wry amusement. Like all the others, he soon came to respect Louis's musical genius; but he was hardly impressed by such demonstrations of musical unsophistication. Jazz history indicates that the personal relationship between Louis Armstrong and Coleman Hawkins was never all that warm, and it is possible that the coolness began here in the early Fletcher Henderson days.

The period of Armstrong's membership of the Henderson band, which lasted just over a year, from October 1924 to November 1925, was however one of formative significance, both for the band and for

Hawkins. Henderson's early work was based largely on the New York dance music of the day, spiced with jazz by the excellent soloists he employed and distinguished by the superior arrangements of himself and Don Redman. Into this fairly stylized music the young Louis Armstrong injected a fierce shot of authentic jazz from the New Orleans seedbed. It brought into the somewhat stiff and jerky idiom common at the time in big bands a rhythmic and melodic fluency and a piquant accentuation which subtly transformed the entire conception and execution. It was perhaps more felt than objectively analysable; but it was there none the less, and it was real. Coleman Hawkins undoubtedly heard and sensed what was happening, and learnt from it. Whatever he may have felt about Louis personally, the impact of Louis's music was certainly not lost upon him.

It has sometimes been argued that, compared to the young Louis Armstrong during these Henderson years, Hawkins's playing was crude and unimaginative, that any contemporary comparison comes down heavily on the side of Armstrong and against Hawkins. This is true; but the reasons for it are not always so readily discussed or analysed. And those reasons amount to precisely this: that whereas Armstrong had an already well established and long since formed tradition of brass playing upon which to draw, and which he could use as a foundation of an original style, there was no such tradition in respect of the saxophone. That was why Coleman Hawkins was obliged to create a foundation technique virtually from scratch before he could properly address himself to the no less demanding task of creating an original style *per se*. Louis Armstrong's phrasing, accentuation, melodic originality and rhythmic subtlety, instinctive as it may have been and almost certainly was, impinged upon the sensitive ears and the creative talent of Coleman Hawkins entirely to his advantage at precisely the time when he was most ready for and in need of it.

It is hardly surprising, then, that during his first years with Henderson, Hawkins was still playing in the familiar staccato and rhythmically turgid style of the time, or that, after Louis Armstrong's stay in the band, he began slowly to evolve his original style on the tenor saxophone. What he does seem to have begun to develop even before that, however, is a full and expressive quality of tone. The huge sound he subsequently managed to build in the body and bell of the tenor was already well past the embryonic stage when he joined Henderson and when he leant an attentive ear to the work of Louis Armstrong. It can be discerned even through the somewhat dim and unfaithful sounds of those old pre-electric recordings, those made, that is, before 1927–8. The staccato phrasing and repetitive dotted rhythms can also be heard there, only too well indeed since the quality of sound tends to emphasize the edges rather than the body of saxophone tone, especially in the lower registers. The alto solos of Don Redman, though thin and somewhat disembodied in tone, tend on the whole to sound more truthful, though even here some allowance has to be made. (It is a curiosity of recording history that the Ellington band was invariably caught better and more truthfully on records than Henderson's, although this did not really come into full and comparative relevance until the end of the 1920s and the beginning of the 1930s.)

It is often assumed that Coleman Hawkins's emergence as a major soloist did not come about until about 1929, or 1928 at the earliest. There is some truth in this, but it is not an assumption to be made out of hand. Without some attention to his earlier work, with or before Fletcher Henderson, complete understanding of the style he did create is bound to be an assessment with an element missing. He himself denied that he was the first to play jazz on the tenor saxophone, but he did admit that from the beginning he was creating an original style. Precisely what that style was and how it evolved can only be judged in the light of his whole career, beginning to end, taking proper note of what he did or tried to do before his full emergence. He did not, like one or two others, Johnny Hodges apparently, spring forth fully armed. He had a hard and quite a long road to travel before he attained the status of an assured master.

The citing of Hodges as an example may, on the face of it, seem a contradiction of the claim that the saxophone had no established tradition of either style or technique and therefore that both had to be created before the master could emerge, as in the case of Coleman Hawkins. But Hodges played alto, and the alto was, as the 'standard' member of the saxophone family, always better established; and in any case Johnny Hodges sprang fully armed from the head of Sidney Bechet, and Bechet played soprano based on the fully formed tradition of the clarinet. Nothing is ever quite as simple or simply explainable as it may appear or as we would like it to be. Whichever way one looks at it, Hawkins with the tenor had a different problem and needed a different means of dealing with it.

Among early Henderson records featuring Hawkins, there are one or two glimpses of the power and the glory to come. But most are undistinguished through awkwardly interjected staccato breaks or short solos of little distinction. Hawkins said later that he developed his big tone to enable the reed section to balance the brass; but it seems more likely that it was the way he was going, and had to go, in any case. It was the age of big-toned instrumentalists – Armstrong, Nanton, Hodges, Carney, Bechet, Dodds, etc. It was much later that the fashion for the pale, in some ways 'purer', instrumental tone took over, and even then it did not last that long. It was Lester Young, of course, who radically altered the bias of tone in the tenor saxophone; but by that time the big tone created by Hawkins had reigned for a decade and more.

As well as the development of his big tone, Hawkins was for some years under the urgent necessity of freeing himself from the tyranny of the beat. Nearly all his solos before 1929, and a good few afterwards, were so heavily dependent on the beat that they were altogether earthbound. The fluidity of his later work, especially his ballad playing, had to be bought. He certainly worked hard for it: he used to say that while the other members of the band were out on the town enjoying themselves he was home practising. This calls to mind Oscar Peterson's description of how his family had to use physical force to remove him from the piano stool at night so that they could get some sleep.

It is necessary to listen to the early Henderson records to get the flavour of Hawkins's first moves in the game of stylistic innovation. But although he was a member of the Henderson band all the while, some of his best recorded work of the late 1920s and early 1930s was done in other contexts. One of these was Red McKenzie's Mound City Blue Blowers, where he appears alongside that quirky genius of the clarinet Pee Wee Russell, with Glenn Miller on trombone, on the famous session of 14 November 1929, which produced the contrasting *Hello, Lola* and *One Hour*, the first fast and still not under tight control, the second slow and in the Hawkins ballad style which led, a decade later, to the most famous of all his records, the 1939 *Body and Soul*. *One Hour*, better known by its fuller title *If I could be with you (one hour tonight)*, has been called the first truly great recorded jazz tenor saxophone solo. By this time Coleman Hawkins had evolved and very nearly perfected the ballad style that constituted one side of his domination of the tenor scene for well over a decade. It has all the poise, the confidence, the unexaggerated mastery of a man who knew precisely what he was doing and why he was doing it. Tone, melodic inventiveness, harmonic and rhythmic compatibility, all combined to make a small masterpiece of

1 The Hawk outside Shakespeare's birthplace, with Bill Harty, 1934
  (Melody Maker)

jazz improvization which might still be improved upon but already set a standard by which all future work in that area, his own included, had to be judged. *Lola* represents the bustling, bursting-at-the seams Hawkins, the other side of the current coin. It is not so masterful, has still some awkwardnesses of rhythm and phrasing, some technical maladroitness seen in the larger retrospect of Hawkins' achievement as a whole; yet it also has a personal force and a foreshadowing of that magisterial quality that was to set him apart from other tenor players.

Around the same time Hawkins made records with a pick-up group known as the Chocolate Dandies – in personnel Henderson-derived – in which he plays, in the December 1930 sessions alongside Benny Carter and the pioneering trombonist from the Henderson ranks, Jimmy Harrison. On them Hawkins can be heard among his peers. Not yet was he the complete master, the voice of absolute authority; but that state is approaching, and it can be heard perhaps more clearly here than on the contemporary records of the Henderson band itself, notably on *Dee Blues, Goodbye Blues* and a fast but controlled *Bugle Call Rag*.

There was also that fine band known as McKinney's Cotton Pickers with which Hawkins recorded in the late 1920s. The Cotton Pickers were originally formed by drummer William McKinney in Detroit in 1926 and were taken over by Don Redman, who left Henderson for the purpose, in 1928. The lineup under Redman was impressive, with Rex Stewart, Joe Smith and Sidney de Paris (t), Cuffy Davidson and Quentin Jackson (tb), with Redman himself leading the reeds and tenor saxophonist Prince Robinson alongside him. Robinson never achieved the fame or the stature of Coleman Hawkins, but he was by no means a slap-tonguing tyro on his instrument. Hawkins himself paid tribute to Robinson.

The departure of Redman left a big hole in the Henderson ranks, a hole which was never quite filled and was ultimately one of the causes of the Henderson band's decline. For the Cotton Pickers records Redman used to 'borrow' some of Henderson's men, and Coleman Hawkins was one who appeared especially at the time, either side of 1930, when Henderson himself was virtually a stranger to the recording studio. Hawkins plays well enough on the Cotton Pickers sessions, though none of the sides show him off at his contemporary best. There was a certain amount of to-ing and fro-ing between Henderson's band and Redman's, but Hawkins, though he recorded with the latter stayed officially on the Henderson payroll.

Between 1923 and 1930 the Fletcher Henderson band played at the Roseland Ballroom in New York. This residency became for a time almost as famous as Duke Ellington's at the Cotton Club or Chick Webb's at the Savoy Ballroom later. Coleman Hawkins recalled that it was a 'stomping band' which played primarily for dancing and that some numbers would last for twenty minutes or so with everyone taking solos in turn as they felt like it. Since all this was long before the advent of the long-playing record it meant that much of the band's recorded work did not faithfully represent what it was doing out in the field. This, combined with Henderson's almost legendary inability (or lack of inclination) to impose even rudimenary discipline, too often resulted in loss of patience on the part of record company managers and broadcasting network directors. It was hard enough for black bands to get lucrative radio dates in any case, most of the plums going to the more favoured white bands; but Henderson's frequent and apparently incurable inability to achieve clean starts and finishes undoubtedly reacted against him. He was in every sense a nice guy and a gifted musician, but he was also a bad manager and a poor leader of men in the hard world of entertainment, so that many chances were lost. The reasons behind his absences from the recording studio around 1930 surely have its origins here.

Hawkins himself appears to have liked working with Henderson and respected him as man and musician. But he too was aware of the shortcomings. Unlike Duke Ellington or Count Basie in their different styles Henderson was not an effective band pianist. He was an excellent accompanist, and in the 1920s he made many records as accompanist to some of the top blues and vaudeville singers, including Bessie Smith. But with the band he was not decisive or forthright enough. It was never in his nature or temperament to be so, and as band leader it simply led to confusion and disarray. Around 1926 Fats Waller would sometimes sit in for recording dates; and Hawkins was not the only one to think, and say, that whenever Fats was on the piano stool the band showed a new and newly infectious enthusiasm. Hawkins said, quite bluntly: 'I didn't think Fletcher was taking advantage of it like he should have done. If it had been me, I'd have hired Fats.' So the process of drift continued and it harmed morale. Fortunately, Coleman Hawkins was always pretty self-possessed, his own morale reasonably self-supporting, so that these and other difficulties did not worry him overmuch. At all events, he stayed with Henderson and held the tenor chair for well over a decade which is an uncommonly long time in the band business. Only some of Ellington's men showed similar tenacity.

Meanwhile, the recording activity continued and Hawkins's musical evolution with it. A couple of tracks cut on 3 October 1930, *Chinatown, my Chinatown* and *Somebody loves me*, have Hawkins very near peak form, though lacking the ultimate in consistency, while a session on 19 March 1931 produced four good numbers, with ripe tenor saxophone work, an excellent clarinet solo on *Hot and Anxious* and an interjection on bass saxophone in *Clarinet Marmalade*. A series of recordings under the title Connie's Inn Orchestra continued the process.

Aside from the Henderson band Hawkins did another session with Mound City Blue Blowers, on 30 June 1931, this time with Muggsy Spanier on cornet and Jimmy Dorsey on clarinet and alto saxophone, plus Eddie Condon with his banjo. A beautifully phrased and poised ballad in the best Hawkins romantic style comes with *Georgia on my mind* and another on *I can't believe that you're in love with me*. Again, as with the earlier Blue Blowers session, the tracks are divided half slow and half fast. A long solo in *Darktown Strutters' Ball* points the way ahead to the power-driving Hawkins of the mature years.

Moving on to 1933, two entirely different setups reveal the Hawk in virtually full emergence. The first brought into being the Henry Allen-Coleman Hawkins partnership, the second what was originally known as Spike Hughes and his Negro Orchestra but subsequently became changed, out of excessive touchiness (since when has it been a matter for shame to call a man or an orchestra 'Negro' when he or it clearly is?) to Spike Hughes and his All-American Orchestra, a more slippery and disagreeably shifty appelation. No matter – both aggregations resulted in some splendid jazz, though in very different contexts.

The pairing of Henry 'Red' Allen and Coleman Hawkins suggested some interesting possibilities, quite a few of which were realized in the studio. Allen, a brilliant, flamboyant and sometimes erratic trumpet player, was currently in the Henderson band and was later to become one of the stars of Luis Russell's. The first two sessions have Dicky Wells on trombone (the third has Benny Morton). Between the second and third session, in September, there is one under Hawkins's sole leadership, though in fact the lineup is virtually the same, with Allen on trumpet but this time J. C. Higginbotham on trombone. All four sessions show Hawk in fine form, the music a kind of easy freewheeling jazz, sometimes slow and reflective, sometimes robust and forceful. In the former Hawkins continues to deploy and develop his rhapsodic style on numbers like *The Day You Came Along* and *Heartbreak Blues* (both from the September session, in the latter his thrusting, full-toned blowing shows an increasing subtlety of rhythm and a power of swing (by no means the same thing), most notably on *Dark Clouds* and *You're Gonna Lose Your Gal*, with some impressive medium style improvising on tunes such as *Ain't Cha Got Music?*. Overall these Allen-Hawkins sessions produced some infectiously good jazz.

The Spike Hughes sessions were something different. They divide into two basic types of music, the first devoted to full band arrangements, mostly of Hughes's own compositions, plus a couple of more or less straight 'jam session' numbers on which Henry Allen and Dicky Wells again feature somewhat in the style of the earlier Allen-Hawkins records. On some of the Hughes numbers Hawk is joined by the most gifted of his tenor saxophone disciples, Leon 'Chu' Berry, though there is no suggestion of anything approaching a cutting contest. Hawkins dominates virtually throughout. Berry has sometimes been called Hawkins's nearest and most dangerous rival, but that is only superficially true: what is nearer the mark is that Berry's early death, like that of Herschel Evans, deprived the Hawkins school of tenor playing of some of its most valuable support when it was most out of fashion, during the late 1940s and early 1950s, leaving only Ben Webster to maintain the bulwarks and hold the bridge when the Lester Young approach was all the rage among junior aspirants.

Patrick C. 'Spike' Hughes is a distinguished writer, critic and composer of Irish descent who in his youth was one of the leading figures on the British jazz scene, as double-bass player and arranger. Indeed, he is credited with having invented the 'slap' technique on bass. After working and recording in London, he went to the US in 1933 and there produced a series of original jazz compositions which have long since become classics. The 'Negro Orchestra' he used for the purpose was basically the band Benny Carter was fronting at the time, and it was hearing Carter's music with his band that provoked him to write his own compositions and arrangements. The Carter outfit was augmented by one or two outside musicians, notably Henry Allen and Coleman Hawkins, and it is Hawkins, Allen and Dicky Wells who share the major solo honours. Hughes also made good use of the flute of Wayman Carver, a fairly innovatory move, anticipating the passion for the flute which came in with the 'cool' jazz of the 1950s.

In numbers like *Arabesque, Nocturne, Air in D flat* and the beautiful *Donegal Cradle Song* Hughes created music that was both original and of exceptional quality. In fact, the argument could be advanced and defended that in composed jazz these Hughes sessions produced music nowhere excelled outside the best works of Duke Ellington. And much of the distinction of the performances derives from the solo interpretations of Coleman Hawkins. It is fair to say that here, in these Spike Hughes sessions, Hawkins produced some of the finest work of his career, work he sometimes equalled later but never in purely musical terms surpassed. So perfect was his understanding of Hughes's intentions and his execution of them that Hughes later insisted that his contributions to *Donegal Cradel Song* in particular should be permanently written into the score, since 'no other was possible or desirable'.

It was in 1933 also that Hawkins recorded, at different sessions, two of his finest and most famous numbers – *The Talk of the Town* (22 September) and *I've Got to Sing a Torch Song* (3 October), the latter nominally with Horace Henderson and His Orchestra but in fact it was still brother Fletcher's. These two special Hawkins feature numbers remain among the classics of his work, and therefore of all jazz. There have always been those who argue that Hawkins's romantic rhapsodic style introduced an alien and largely inimical element into jazz and that it was a fundamentally degenerate evolution. But these are mostly those of a self-styled 'purist' persuasion who believe that jazz should have stayed with the New Orleans classic style, certainly not later than King Oliver, forgetting both that Oliver himself went on to produce a more evolved and sophisticated kind of jazz, and that any artform that stays permanently locked into one style or period can only die there. The romantic style of ballad playing that Hawkins evolved, though not only he did it, was an extension and essential expansion of the resources of jazz and its own latent potentiality without which it would have remained in a social and cultural backwater.

It is also sometimes argued that these solos of Coleman Hawkins are or tend to be shapeless or formless. But, while it may be true that some of Hawkins's solos do lose their way from time to time, and mistake decoration for structural matter, this is true of most artists in one manner or another, certainly of improvizing jazz musicians who may well be led down byways and into irrelevances in the heat of the moment. Coleman Hawkins, however, was one of the most gifted in this respect, a man and musician who usually maintained a firmer hold on the structure of his solos than the majority who address themselves to the demanding task of extended improvization.

1934 was Hawkins's last year with Fletcher Henderson. For some time the Henderson band had been finding the going hard. The Depression did not help, any more than it helped anyone else. But Fletcher Henderson was not in any case of the metal to 'ride out the deepening Depression', as Benny Goodman, who was so fitted, put it. Also, after the loss of Don Redman to McKinney's Cotton Pickers, Henderson was without a first-class arranger on any permanent basis. His own arranging abilities, which were ironically to bring fame and fortune to Benny Goodman a year or so later, were only just beginning to emerge in full spate. He picked up the call-and-response style used by Redman and turned it into a leading principle, which again was a major contribution to the world-wide success of the Goodman band. But Goodman was, and remains, a tough, hard-headed, totally unsentimental man of business and music, while Fletcher Henderson was always a nice guy who inspired loyalty and affection but was something of an incurable innocent in the hard world, especially the economically embattled world of the Depression years.

The Henderson band did not break up before Hawkins left it; that came a year or two later. Nor is there any direct evidence that the way things were clearly going determined Hawkins' departure. Certainly, he was concerned about the band's lowering musical standards, the way Henderson was relying more and more on borrowed scores so that, in his own words, 'finally the band, to me, got to the place where it sounded just like other bands, which is no good. We used to play numbers that sounded like the Casa Loma band at times, because we had gangs of their arrangements.' Hawkins recognised that it was the loss of Redman that had led to the situation arising in the first place. Redman left in 1927, so the rundown took some time to work through. Also, the quality of the soloists, Hawkins himself, Jimmy Harrison, Joe Smith, Rex Stewart, Bobby Stark and others, helped offset the too often poor quality of the scores. Then Henderson brought Benny Carter in with his multi-instrumental skills and his imaginative arrangements; but it was not on a permanent enough basis, and in any case economic conditions in the band world were rapidly deteriorating. Henderson kept going into 1935, but it was clear before then that all was not well – not least to Coleman Hawkins.

During the Spike Hughes sessions there had been no rivalry and no

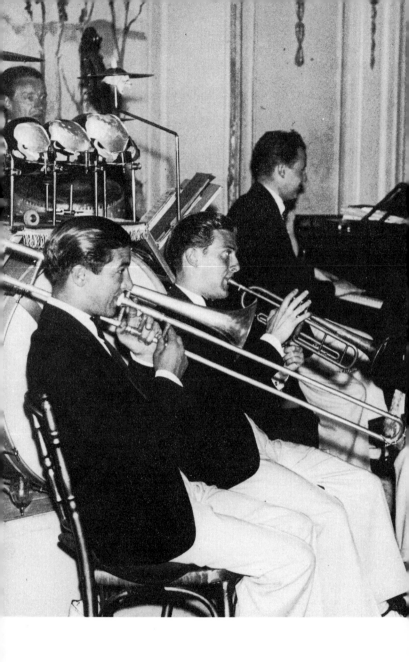

2 Hawkins with The Ramblers in Europe, mid-1930s (Melody Maker)

attempts at cutting between Hawkins and Chu Berry. But Hawk in fact was always ready for a good contest, a standup fight with other saxophonists. His stature by 1934 was such that few sought the battle and those who did usually found themselves reduced. But it was not quite always like that. Once it turned out the other way. There are several accounts of what happened, including one, by pianist and arranger/composer the late Mary Lou Williams, which appears to be the most authoritative. It happened like this: the Henderson band had fulfilled a one-night stand in Kansas City and then moved on for another the next night in St Louis (after finishing his seven-year stint at the Roseland Ballroom, Henderson took the band on the road and toured for the next three years). But Coleman Hawkins had heard some talk about the roughnecking Kaycee saxophonists and so stayed on after the official engagement to see what it was all about. He soon discovered. He went to the Cherry Blossom to settle a few musical accounts. As soon as the news got round that the great Hawk was in town, the place began to fill with saxophone players, among them Lester Young, Ben Webster, and Herschel Evans. A battle of giants ensued and went on into the small hours of the morning. In the way of such contests, each man would purloin a phrase from someone else and proceed to send it up. In the end, despite everything that Hawk could do – and he put all of himself into out-blowing the Kaycee upstarts – he was bested. Lester Young was pronounced the winner, the man who, by another irony, was some years later temporarily to displace Hawkins from his throne as king of the tenor saxophone. Never before had Hawkins lost out in a cutting contest, and he was not often to lose again. But this time he did. The last part of the legend is that he burnt out the engine of his brand new Cadillac making for St Louis and the next Henderson date.

In fact 'cutting contests' are by no means uncommon in musical history. There are many stories from the past of such encounters, including at least one where Beethoven picked up a part from a rival's string quartet, looked at it, put it face downwards on the piano top, and proceeded to improvize brilliantly on a phrase from it for at least an hour, scattering all opposition. The age of Franz Liszt was also a notable one for public battles at the piano. The jazz variety is therefore only following historical precedent.

Outwardly, Hawkins's departure from the Henderson ranks came about by accident. It appears to have happened as a result of a chance remark he made to a former colleague in the Henderson band, bass player June Cole, that he would like to visit Europe. Cole, who had recently been there himself, suggested that Hawk contact Jack Hylton in London, since Hylton ran a major band and was also a leading impresario. Hawkins took the advice, cabled Hylton, and received a good offer by return. It turned out as simple as that, and for the next five years Coleman Hawkins, already recognized all over the States and widely in Europe through his records as the greatest living tenor saxophone player, almost on a par with Louis Armstrong himself, made his personal impact beyond the US. However, unlike Armstrong he was not a showman, so that his reputation was more restricted to the ranks of the jazz aficionados and made small appeal to the larger public which had come to sit (and pay) at Louis's feet. Yet where it mattered, Hawk's reputation stood as high as any.

Just before he left the US Hawkins made a series of recordings in February and March 1934. On 2 February he sat in with a Benny Goodman group and cut four sides, including a new version of *Georgia on my Mind* and one of *Junk Man*, the number made famous in the Jack Teagarden recording, with harpist Caspar Reardon. It was not a great session, but it produced some agreeable music and certainly did not disgrace Hawkins.

On 6 March came his last official recording with Fletcher Henderson, for Victor. Hawkins is in relaxed and masterful form, notably on *Hocus Pocus* and *Tidal Wave*, the latter in particular showing Hawkins's now complete command of soloing at a very fast tempo, little left of the old staccato barking except where positively required. Then, last of all, came a curious session on 8 March, with only pianist Buck Washington as accompanist. It is not altogether successful, though Evensmo's strictures are really myopic. It contains a very good *On the Sunny Side of the Street*; on the other hand, either the combination of tenor saxophone and piano only is inherently unsatisfactory or it had not been thoroughly worked through and out by the time the session took place. Or perhaps it was simply that Washington was not quite good enough a pianist. Good he was, but not a Hines or a James P. Johnson or a Fats Waller, any of whom, as well as one or two others, might have provoked Hawkins to extend himself just that necessary bit further. The Armstrong/Hines duo partnership tells another story.

This was to be the end of Coleman Hawkins's American recording and musical activities for just over five years. But it was certainly not to be the end of his overall activities, or the interruption to his now established fame that some must have feared. In every way it marked an increase in both.

He sailed in the liner *Île de France* and arrived in England on Good Friday, 29 March 1934.

The European

Exactly why Coleman Hawkins decided to leave the US just when his reputation was at its height has never been completely explained. Hawkins himself, a naturally taciturn man when it came to his private affairs, never gave more than a few conventional clues. One of the reasons he left Henderson seems to be because of the uncertainties, both musical and economic, that were undermining the band; but his reasons for going to Europe, and staying there for all but five years, appear to have been both simpler and more complex. It may in the first place have been as uncomplicated as that he just fancied the idea and thought he would like a trip to Europe. But, underneath, the currents obviously ran deeper.

Many feared that his isolation from the American jazz scene would have a depressing effect on Hawkins's musical development. He was already acclaimed the master, the undisputed king of the tenor saxophone. But the king needs courtiers of some quality if he is to retain his throne. In Europe Hawkins would be playing with, from the strictly jazz standpoint, inferior musicians. The stimulus of sitting in with his peers on other instruments is always good for a musician in any context – it is good for anyone whoever they may be or whatever their area of operations– and there are plenty of cases of jazzmen who have been felt not to do themselves justice in poor musical company. Bix Beiderbecke is the classic and often quoted example of this, and at the end of his life Sidney Bechet's tremendous vitality and creativeness was sapped by continual playing with third-rate French trad. bands. Thus the fear that Hawkins was doing himself no musical good by transfering to Europe might well have been justified. That it turned out not to be justified was due to a number of reasons.

One reason was that he was not the only expatriate among jazz musicians. Other Americans were around, notably in Paris including Benny Carter and Bill Coleman. In addition, many American musicians, like Dicky Wells, were visitors to Paris and recorded there. Beyond that again, the European jazz musicians were learning their business, and a number of good bands and groups were emerging and, if not of unimpeachable quality in their own right, were quite capable of providing substantial support for their natural superiors. And there was at least one European jazz musician of unquestioned originality, the Belgian guitarist Django Reinhardt, with whom Hawkins recorded in the mid-1930s. Reinhardt's reputation may have become a little exaggerated in the mist of time and the pulls of nostalgia, but there is no doubt that he was a genuinely original talent whose contributions as soloist to many recordings of the period lifted them out of an inevitable mediocrity; and this, includes, even if it is heresy to say so, many of the Quintet of the Hot Club of France, the undisputed vogue in those days. Overall, however, Coleman Hawkins found Europe and European musicians congenial and in no way did his genius decline. On the contrary, perhaps to some initial surprise, it actually increased in scope and potential.

His European venture did not start on a particularly good note. He was, as we have seen, brought into the Jack Hylton organization. Immediately after his arrival in England Hylton intended to present him in a big show business spectacular with Louis Armstrong, who was also currently appearing in England under Hylton's auspices. But everything went wrong. There was a huge press build-up; but then at the last moment Louis withdrew. The circumstances are still somewhat obscure, but the result was a series of false press reports, public misleadings, and a certain amount of bitterness all round. At the time, most of the blame was attributed to Armstrong, and later attempts to exonerate him, including his own, were never quite convincing. Also, knowing Coleman Hawkins's nature and deportment it is unlikely that he would have walked out on any engagement. Nor for that matter was it Louis's custom so to do. On the other hand, it does seem that something upset Louis and made him literally walk out on the date at the last moment. Just why he did so is not easily explained by reference to contemporary reports or from objective analysis. A good deal of the trouble as Louis himself later intimated, was due to the press jumping a number of guns and generally making unwarranted assumptions. Louis seems to have welcomed Hawkins's arrival in England, but then had second thoughts. In fairness it must be said that Louis's own reception by the English musical press was not exactly ecstatic. He was accused of purveying '50 per cent showmanship, 50 per cent instrumental cleverness, about nought per cent music'. Louis did take note and recognized that his most faithful and knowledgeable English followers wanted his best music not his pyrotechnical nonsense, and subsequently he mended his ways; all the same, the censure cannot have made him feel any happier or more secure. At the same time, according to the authoritative biography by Max Jones and John Chilton, he was having trouble with his tour

3 Coleman Hawkins, mid-1930s (Melody Maker)

management: John Collins, who had brought him over, returned to the States and Jack Hylton took over. When Hylton arranged the Armstrong/ Hawkins spectacular, Louis may well have felt he was being exploited. Also, he was not at all sure that he could switch roles quickly enough to ensure that he did both himself and Hawk justice. One wonders, too, if there may not have been beneath the surface some lingering needle from the old days when Louis was a social if not a musical tyro in the Fletcher Henderson band, some remnant, in the subconscious at least, of a feeling of personal inferiority. Whatever the true reason, the great London meeting of giant talents never did take place.

While in London Hawk recorded four titles accompanied by Stanley Black (p), Albert Harris (g) and Tiny Winters (b). The session, on 18 November 1934, produced pleasant music, the kind that may not shake any foundations but has a quality of equanimity which proclaims the hand of a master at work. All the tunes are familiar jazz standards, including *Lady Be Good* and *Honeysuckle Rose*, and the majestic Hawk rides high all through, mixing passages of imaginative improvizing with others of a more straightforward but no less authoritative character. What the session really demonstrates is that Hawkins had reached that stage in his personal evolution when he would always dominate in any company except the very highest and, whatever the level of lesser company, his own stature would be undiminished. This was a considerable accomplishment in itself: not only did it banish fears that by going to Europe he might be tempted into lowering his standards to those of his musical surroundings, on the more positive side it also demonstrated that he had reached the stage where his mastery of both style and technique were not dependent upon setting but created its own. Of the pre-Parker saxophonists perhaps only Johnny Hodges had a similar ability to rise above his surroundings and maintain perfect identity. This from Hawkins's point of view was to be extremely important, not only during the next four years in Europe but no less after the 'bop' eruption when the context for all active jazzmen was radically altered.

The first months of 1935 found Coleman Hawkins active in Holland and France. In The Hague on 4 February, he undertook his first recording session with the Dutch band known as The Ramblers. This was certainly one of the better European bands, able at times even to find the first elements of swing, that elusive quality which lies not only at the heart of good jazz, but in one form or another of all good music, and which was particularly elusive in the non-American jazz of the 1930s.

38

Here, in the first Ramblers session, Hawkins confirms what he had already demonstrated in London, that he could ride and rise above any musical setting in which he found himself. In fact, the Ramblers association was to continue through at least three major recording sessions during his European residence. There is a marvellously assured and relaxed quality about Hawk's playing here in a series of mostly familiar titles which he must have played many times and several of which he recorded more than once, *After You've Gone, I Only Have Eyes for You, I Wish I Were Twins* etc. This first meeting of Coleman Hawkins and The Ramblers seems to have sparked the best from both.

A month later and Hawk was in Paris, making his first French recordings on 2 March with Michael Warlop's orchestra, a group which contained some of France's leading musicians, including Django Reinhardt and Stephane Grappelly (on piano). Also present were those two talented French reed players André Ekyan and Alix Combelle, both of whom reappear frequently on sessions in France with visiting American jazzmen. This first Paris session too was an artistic success. There were three numbers with the full band – a very good rhapsodic *What a Difference a Day Made, Blue Moon* and a lively *Avalon* – and one, *Stardust*, with the rhythm section only.

Overall the Warlop band does not swing as convincingly as The Ramblers at their best. There is too often a sense of chugging in twos that was the bane of the Grappelly/Reinhardt Hot Club performances. Much of this was due to Django Reinhardt. Unquestionably a soloist of genius, Django as rhythm guitarist was too inclined to chug on the beat; he lacked that fluency, that sense of passing one note or phrase on to the next, which is the basis of all good rhythm and certainly the very heart of swing. He has often been praised as a rhythm guitarist, but although he sometimes made notable harmonic and melodic interjections, in the rhythm department, he was no genius. All the same, the contrast between Hawkins's fluency and freedom of line and phrase and the rhythm section's rather static chugging does sometimes make an effective juxtaposition. And whatever one may think about Django's rhythm work, there can be no doubt whatsoever about the marvellous quality of his solos. Here at least is a beautiful foil to the huge tone and confidence of Hawkins.

It is only possible to chart Coleman Hawkins's European years by his recordings. He seems to have played around various European venues during the summer of 1935. The next port of call in the log, so to say, is 26

August, when he did another session with The Ramblers, at Laren. There had been changes in The Ramblers' lineup, most notably the entry into the ranks of trumpet player and composer/arranger Jack Bulterman. Bulterman wrote some original numbers and made some arrangement which particularly suited Hawkins. The result was not necessarily better than the first session, but there is some fine music of an ever maturing vintage, including an excellent *Meditation* and a finely swinging *Chicago* in which the band's swing really does match Hawkins's. The most original number is Bulterman's *Netcha's Dream* which gave Hawk's melodic and harmonic resourcefulness a rather different quality to bite on.

In April 1937 Hawkins recorded four sides with a Swiss group known as The Berries and led by drummer Berry Peritz. The results were surprisingly successful, and even a pretty hectic *Tiger Rag* does not degenerate into shambles. *It May Not be True* has some fine Hawkins, but the curiosity is *Love Cries* which has a Hawkins vocal. It does not suggest that Louis Armstrong or Big Joe Turner, or any other established jazz singer, had much to fear from the possibility that Hawk might develop this side of his genius; indeed, he is said to have stated that the record was issued without his permission and that its only virtue was its obscurity. But this is not quite borne out by a couple of sessions he did at the same time accompanied only by Joe Turner at the piano (not of course Big Joe). In fact, Turner only accompanies Hawkins on the tenor tracks; the rest are taken up by Hawkins singing and accompanying himself at the piano, with another *Love Cries*. These sides seem never to have been issued, but they appear in the listings and constitute a minor curiosity.

A year later came two of the most important of Hawk's European sessions. The first, on 26 April 1937, was his third session with The Ramblers, again at Laren, their home base. This contains some of Hawkins's finest work, covering as it does virtually the entire gamut of his mature style, from the rhapsodic *Consolations* to the up tempo *Original Dixieland One-Step*. Throughout Hawkins delivers himself of musical conceptions and executions which place him as the only rival to Louis Armstrong at that time as the world's premier jazz virtuoso soloist. The final number here, *Something Is Gonna Give Me Away*, has Hawkins with The Ramblers' rhythm section only – or rather The Ramblers' team of Jack Pet (g), F. Feinders (b) and Kees Kranenburg (d) plus Freddy Johnson (p) replacing the band's regular pianist. This is of some interest in demonstrating Hawkins's mature use of that dotted rhythm he was always fond of and had started using with Fletcher Henderson, a kind of musical iambics which became almost one of his trademarks and can still today be heard in the work of many tenor saxophonists.

Two days later he was in Paris, recording with an *ad hoc* group, including Benny Carter on alto and trumpet, under the name of Coleman Hawkins and His All-Star Jam Band. The group itself is a slightly smaller version of the Michael Warlop orchestra Hawkins had used a couple of years earlier. The results, however, are even finer. Of the four numbers recorded, it is hard to pick any one that stands above the others. Perhaps *Honeysuckle Rose* would have it in most connoisseurs' judgment, and it certainly contains one of Hawkins's most justly famous solos, almost equalling the later *Body and Soul* in general repute; but between that, *Out of Nowhere, Crazy Rhythm* and *Sweet Georgia Brown* (not even raped as she too often is by importunate jazzmen in a desperate hurry), it is more than hard to choose. Carter, the musician Coleman Hawkins perhaps admired and respected more than any other, makes superb contributions, and indeed, so successful was the collaboration that Hawkins and Carter tried to recreate their joint achievement some years later, with only partial success; near perfection can seldom be recaptured and recreated. The same rhythm team is operative here as on the earlier date, with Reinhardt on guitar and Grappelly at the piano. Django does not solo, and although there is the same tendency to chug, it seems to inspire Hawkins in particular to yet greater rhythmic freedom and melodic fantasy. The French saxophonists Ekyan and Combelle also make notable contributions. If anyone had lingering doubts that Hawkins's European sojourn would do him musical harm, here must be the final refutation.

Back in Holland for the summer of 1937, Hawkins cut two long solo performances backed by pianist Freddy Johnson in Hilversum on 26 May and two more on 18 August in a session that produced another *Stardust* plus two apparently rejected items. Johnson was an excellent accompanist, if no particularly masterful solo performer. He also appeared in another Benny Carter session which Evensmo gives as taking place in The Hague on the same day with Hawkins. There seems to be a discrepancy here, unless there was a great deal of rushing around, always possible with jazz sessions. However it was, here was another Carter session which produced music of high quality, especially on Carter's own *Mighty Like the Blues*. The groups featured George

41

4 Hawkins the leader, 1940s Melody Maker

Chisholm on trombone in a highly cosmopolitan team which Albert McCarthy, but not Evensmo, said also contained alto saxophonist Bertie King, a gifted West Indian musician. Another exceptional number from the session is the powerful *My Buddy*.

Yet another Coleman Hawkins/Freddy Johnson session, this time with the drummer M. van Cleef took place the following year, on 14 June 1938. This produced six final versions of varying quality, including a rendering of *When Buddah Smiles* later made famous by Benny Goodman in the Fletcher Henderson arrangement (one of his very best): it sounds a bit thin and peculiar stripped down to tenor saxophone, piano and drums. All in all, this is definitely Hawkins's session: Johnson plays adequately, but the drummer is expendable, so it was left to Hawk to fly high and keep the performance from remaining earthbound. It is an even more than usually curate's eggish session.

Hawkins's European stay was now drawing to an end. He had been developing his style all the time, and a new, gruffer, more aggressive note had become more and more prominent. Perhaps it was not so much a new element as the coming to the fore of one that had been there all along – one can hear plenty of intimations of it during the Henderson years – but had tended to back off to some extent while the softer, more rhapsodic aspect had been formed and consolidated. But one thing is certain: whatever may have been the fears that troubled his admirers when he left the US, and whatever had been his experiences during his absence, he returned there a riper and more fully mature musician. This probably had little to do with European residence, but was the natural evolution of a major talent, one that would have taken place wherever he had been based during those years. He was essentially a developing musical personality; he never could or would stand still; he needed to evolve, to shed and regrow musicial skins, and he needed continual stimulus to bring it about, as do all such talents. If he had stayed in the States through the latter half of the 1930s, he would have developed just the same, and in virtually the same manner and directions, but it may have taken a different form, or proceeded at a slightly different pace in particular directions.

He returned to England in the early part of 1939. By then the musicians' union ban was operating, so that he was not permitted to undertake professional engagements or make records. The problem was surmounted by a pretty piece of sleight of hand, as hypocritical as one might expect in the circumstances, whereby Hawkins was allowed to tour the country as a demonstrator of Selmer saxophones in the company of an accordionist name of Gerald Crossman. By this ruse kind permission was given for the greatest saxophonist in the world to appear before British audiences; and since it was nominally a publicity tour, no fees for tickets were charged so that those British audiences had a free feast of marvellous music. It was all a sorry wrangle, but at least Hawk did appear. He even by some subterfuge contrived to make a couple of records with Jack Hylton and his Orchestra, rather good ones too.

The clouds of war, temporarily pushed back by the Munich Agreement in 1938, were gathering still more ominously during the summer of 1939. Nothing it seemed then could prevent a huge European tragedy. And none could even begin to guess how far it would spread or how long it would last. No one with sense and without a compelling reason for staying on would want to wait for the storm to break, but whether Coleman Hawkins returned to the States primarily because of the now inescapable threat of war in Europe or for some more complex reason is not known for sure.

Perhaps it was not even known precisely by himself at the time. There are pulls and currents deep in the subconscious which often determine choices and actions apparently taken and made for other reasons by the conscious mind. Hawkins may have felt that it was time for him to go home anyway, that he needed to renew contact with his musical and racial roots for permanent expatriatism is not always good for an artist, especially for a jazz musician whose sources of creative force are fundamentally American. If there had been no threat of war, no Hitler, would the result, the choice have been the same? Coleman Hawkins left Europe and arrived back in New York in mid-July 1939. He returned to Europe many times during the post-war years; but he never again settled there.

5 Publicity still, mid 1940s (Melody Maker)

Bird of Prey

Coleman Hawkins may have been resident in Europe for five years, but he certainly knew what was going on back home in the States. There was trans-Atlantic traffic of musicians and other bearers of information, and he kept in touch. He would have known, therefore, that there was a new tenor saxophone star, a powerful rival for his own crown, and that it was none other than Lester Young, his old conquerer in the famous musical shootout in Kansas City in 1934. It has been claimed that it was after that famous victory that Lestor Young earned the nickname The President, but it remains more likely that it was Billie Holiday who bestowed it on him. Whatever of that, Hawkins returned to find that the gauntlet had been thrown down again in his absence. He lost no time in picking it up.

He was still king in his own domain, at least among musicians, and there is no evidence that he did not welcome the challenge from a player so different from himself in every way, personal as well as artistic. Indeed, although the idiot faction-mongering – 'bop' versus 'swing' and modern v. traditional – that went on in the jazz world in the late 1940s and early 1950s, lead to him suffering from neglect and disillusion, Hawkins probably saw that the challenge was an overall healthy one for the jazz world in general and the tenor saxophone scene in particular. In a sane world, the rise of a new style and approach does not necessarily mean the instant demise of an old and established one. The process should be cumulative not contradictory. The emergence of Lester Young increased the full scope of the tenor saxophone in a manner which should, had sanity prevailed, have been of benefit to everyone concerned. And in fact that is precisely what did happen in the longer run, whatever may have been the case in the short (and short tempered) one.

Hawkins's first recording session after his return was with Lionel Hampton as part of a band which included Benny Carter and Ben Webster on saxophones and young Dizzy Gillespie on trumpet. The main interest from the historical point of view, however, is the rhythm section, which had Charlie Christian on guitar and Milt Hinton on bass plus Cozy Cole on the drums, an immediately pre-bop nucleus. If the music itself is still firmly rooted in the swing era, the underlying current can clearly be felt moving and throwing up ripples for the future. This took place in New York City on 11 September 1939. Four sides were cut, on two of which Hawkins' solos, *When Lights Are Low* and *One Sweet Letter From You*, both show in their differing ways that Hawk is back and is going to stand no nonsense from anyone. He sat in again with Hampton on 21 December. Although Carter is again present, the lineup is otherwise quite different, with Edmond Hall on clarinet, Joe Sullivan (p), Freddie Green (g), Artie Bernstein (b) and Zutty Singleton (d), in general a more familiar grouping to which Hawk responds with great assurance and élan on a version of *Singin' The Blues*, which almost rivals the classic Bix Beiderbecke/Frankie Trumbauer version, a splendid fresh interpretation of *My Buddy*, and a *Dinah* that avoids the temptation to rip the lady's pants off, despite the up tempo and the decisive approach.

In between these Hampton sessions came the most famous date in which Coleman Hawkins ever took part, the one that produced *Body and Soul*, the record which carried his name and fame well beyond the confines of the jazz fraternity with the tune that was ever after associated with his name. His first formal engagement after returning from Europe was at the popular Kelly's Stable club in New York. For this residency he brought together a nine-piece band which did not feature any big names, except perhaps trumpeter Joe Guy, of ominous association with Billie Holiday but still a talented musician. On 11 October 1939, the band went into the RCA Victor studios and recorded four numbers, of which *Body and Soul* appears to have been something of an afterthought. Hawk had been using *Body and Soul* as an encore at Kelly's Stables, sometimes running through an almost indefinite number of choruses. He was not otherwise particularly interested in the tune; it was simply a useful workhorse for sending the Kelly's customers home happy. It seems that Victor A&R man Leonard Joy had heard Hawkins go through the *Body and Soul* routine on several occasions and had been impressed. He accordingly asked Hawkins to put it on to disc. Hawk was still unenthusiastic but in the end agreed to the request. The result must have astonished everyone, Hawkins himself not least. Thus do classics and best sellers often come about, not by deliberate choice or calculation, but on the inspiration or prompting of the moment and more or less by accident.

The success of *Body and Soul* is in many respects surprising. Although it came out unusually well on the day, it did not represent any particular new quality in Hawk's style or technique. He had been playing that way for years; one could look back through his discography and find many examples of his rhapsodic manner in this type of number, including at least one *Stardust*. And his solo delivery on Spike Hughes's *Donegal Cradle Song* was probably superior. But *Body and Soul* caught on and became a puzzling success.

Hawkins's own account reflects that puzzlement. 'I didn't want to record it at all,' he said later. 'I just played it through once and made up the ending when I got to it. That's the one record I don't understand. It's the first and only record I ever heard of that all the squares dig as well as the jazz people.' He must have felt at the time rather like Miles Davis felt after he had been suddenly acclaimed at Newport in 1955, reflecting in some understandable surprise that he had been playing the same way for several years so what was all the fuss about?

That *Body and Soul* is beautifully constructed and played with total mastery hardly needs stressing; yet both the technical mastery and the structural cohesion are by no means unique in Hawkins's work and were not new even at the time. The rest of that session produced good Hawkins work, if nothing quite so perfectly turned as *Body and Soul*. Evensmo suggests that *Fine Dinner* marks the beginning of the 'honking-tenor', a device more immediately associated with Lester Young who developed it alongside the rhythmic rat-tat-tatting on one note which he brought to his instrumental style from his early days as a drummer.

After this and before the second Hampton session, Hawk did a set with a group containing his favourite musical colleague Benny Carter and with the clarinettist Danny Polo who had worked for many years in England during the 1920s and 1930s, most of them as a member of the Ambrose Orchestra. This group answered to the name of the Varsity Seven and produced four numbers associated with Louis Armstrong and New Orleans, including *Save It Pretty Mama* and *It's Tight Like That* (slight title variation) and *Easy Rider*.

1940 was a busy year for Hawkins. On 3 January he undertook another record session with a group which again included Carter and Polo, with the powerful J.C. Higginbotham on trombone. This produced some top-class music, including a very fine *When Day Is Done*, plus versions of *The Sheik of Araby* and *My Blue Heaven* not far behind and a jaunty *Bouncing With Bean* which may well be the first use of Hawkins's nickname 'Bean' to appear in a tune title on a record label. A second Varsity Seven session had Joe Turner (Big Joe this time) as singer and again contains top class Hawkins. On 30 January he made four more sides with the band Benny Carter was currently fronting which brought

49

a find *Slow Freight* and an underrated *Fish Fry*.

An interesting session on 25 May found Hawkins teamed with Roy Eldridge and yet again Benny Carter for an informal session that in some ways harked back to the famous Coleman Hawkins-Henry Allen sessions of 1933. 'Little Jazz' was not always the most reliable partner for Hawkins; his exuberance, which could sometimes bubble over, was not above provoking Hawk into retaliation and a consequent descent into perpetrated vulgarities, as was to happen a few times later on. But this session, under the revived name of The Chocolate Dandies, contained some richly contoured music, with two Hawkins specialities, *I Surrender Dear* and *Dedication* outstanding. Roy Eldridge was also present on a broadcast jam session held in Martin Block's Make Believe Ballroom. It was not a setting of the kind that Hawkins ever really favoured or shone in. Again, it tended to provoke him into over-blowing and general musical rough-necking.

Throughout 1940 Hawkins was leading a big band playing in the swing idiom which began its career at the end of 1939 at the Golden Gate Ballroom and then went on countrywide tours. But the band, though it appears to have had excellent qualities and came together as a unit, was not a commercial success and soon broke up. Hawkins himself does not appear to have relished the role of band leader. The job of leading a big band is not one that sits easily on everyone's shoulders. It is not a question of musical ability – some very gifted and very famous musicians have not succeeded at it, Johnny Hodges being one. It is an extremely demanding task which requires particular qualities that have nothing much to do with music. One might legitimately say, adopting the well-known Peter principle that everyone reaches their level of incompetence, that some jazz musicians reach it when they set out on the hazardous business of band leading. What was true of Johnny Hodges was also true of Jack Teagarden, the general opinion then being that he was too nice a guy for such an occupation. Coleman Hawkins did not in fact lead a big band for more than one brief period; whether he thereafter avoided doing it again because he was unsure of his ability to succeed, or simply because he did not fancy it, is an open question.

His big band – which had some good players, including trumpeters Joe Guy and Tommy Stevenson, trombonists Claude Jones and Sandy Williams, and drummer J.C. Heard – undertook one studio recording session for Okeh, on 9 August 1940, which produced a somewhat violent but exciting *Rocky Comfort* and a pleasant *Serenade to a Sleeping Beauty*, a typical piece of Hawkins romanticism. After this, Hawkins contented himself for the rest of his life with fronting small groups, and few of those on a permanent basis.

Another Commodore session during 1943 (not 1940 as indicated on one record sleeve) has Cootie Williams on trumpet and Art Tatum at the piano, with Ed Hall (cl), Al Casey (g), Oscar Pettiford (b) and Sid Catlett (d). This is an even more intriguing session than the earlier one. It has one Hawkins original, *Mop Mop*, and two tunes by Leonard Feather *Esquire Bounce* and *Esquire Blues*. The lineup is interesting, and although Cootie is not at his fiercest and Tatum is comparatively restrained the music certainly comes to life, with Pettiford's bass hinting at the new rhythmic patterns of the emerging bop era.

Through the first half of the 1940s, while bop was conquering and the jazz world was preparing to split itself into warring factions – the so-called 'revivalists' on the one hand, the boppers on the other, with the main body of musicians of the swing era caught in the crossfire – Coleman Hawkins pursued a lordly and more or less omnipotent course. Despite the formidable challenge of Lester Young, he was still king of the tenor saxophone. This position he retained partly because it was impossible to deny it to him on purely technical grounds, partly because his advanced harmonic sense and general musical literacy enabled him to talk to and consort with the modernists on their own terms. During these early 1940s he continued to play mostly with his musical contemporaries, but all the time he took note of what was going on around him and introduced elements of it into his own playing. On occasions, too, he used some of the young modernists on his club dates and even at times on his recordings. In 1944 he was the first to feature Thelonious Monk on a record session.

For the time being he went his own way and the jazz world applauded and paid him homage. He and Lester Young divided the honours, their styles so contrasted that only blind prejudice and blatant stupidity could find reason why they should not coexist on the same scene. Indeed during these first years of the 1940s, he was as busy with engagements and recording sessions as at any time in his career. In April he sat in as guest on recordings by the Count Basie and the Benny Goodman bands, each time producing good if not startlingly original work. In both cases, however, the results were much superior to that on a Metronome All-Star Band session of three months earlier. As usual with such cases, the all-star band never gets near to any form of cohesion and is mostly a

51

6 Dave Dexter's International Jazzmen in 1945 with (l-r): Hawk, John
Kirby, Bill Coleman, Max Roach, Nat King Cole, Buster Bailey,
Benny Carter and (foreground) Oscar Moore (Melody Maker)

succession of unrelated solos in a thoroughly rabble-rousing style. Hawkins here tends to honk away like an angry goose on the run.

The big band swing era, now drawing to an end, had popularized a certain form of jazz, led by the world-wide acclaim for the Benny Goodman orchestra; but many felt that this popularity was increasingly a kind of prostitution of true jazz, at best a dilution of its innermost spirit in the interests of a growing commercialism. Duke Ellington is reported to have said: 'Jazz is music, Swing is business', and Goodman himself seems to have come, if subconsciously, to much the same conclusion. He formed his small groups with the main band to play 'purer' jazz and so set a fashion for most of the other swing bands, many of which featured small jazz groups as 'bands within a band'. Coleman Hawkins was only incidentally involved in the big swing band scene, and he was among the first to take advantage of the small specialist record labels which sprang up at this time. He actually made the first recordings for the new Apollo label, with a band heavily featuring bop musicians and brought together by Dizzy Gillespie. His natural idiom was still a modified kind of 'mainstream,' his preferred colleagues those of his own generation musically and biologically; but he was never afraid to branch out into the new fast-running current. His own style had progressed in harmonic awareness and had taken on a more aggressive quality, also in keeping with the general mood of the times, which was in the process of rejecting the increasingly bland style of the swing era and substituting a more passionate and committed involvement.

On the other hand, there was another modern school evolving, and one with which Coleman Hawkins had little in common and little musical sympathy. This was the 'cool' school which came to a head in 1949 with the Miles Davis/Gerry Mulligan scene-shifting session known collectively as 'The Birth of the Cool'. The 'cool' had been brewing underneath for sometime, often under a number of mis-apprehensions, but it came to final definition with the Davis/Mulligan sessions, using instrumentations extending the normal range for a jazz orchestra and owing much to the pioneering instrumentation of the Claude Thornhill orchestra.

It was this school or movement which as much as anything caused Coleman Hawkins and others of his musical style and persuasion to be cast out of fashion and into a period of almost total neglect. It was not so much the original boppers who displaced the men of Hawkins's type and character as the 'cool' school. Miles Davis himself had been pre-eminent in the earlier Charlie Parker groups, his style still then unformed and certainly in complete contrast to the exuberant and high flying music of Dizzy Gillespie. Davis was not a virtuoso and never has been. He evolved an original and potent style, but at first, in the Parker days he seemed to have difficulty in getting his music out.

On the saxophone scene things were a little different, though hardly less ominous for the old guard who became dubbed with the stigma, as it came to be seen, of the swing era, in many cases quite unjustifiably. Coleman Hawkins was certainly so dubbed and he went not only totally out of fashion during the late 1940s and the early 1950s; he seems under the pressures of the time to have lost direction and confidence too. It was not a permanent condition and by the later 1950s he was restored, and had restored himself, to a position of prominence in his profession.

The style of Lester Young is generally regarded as the antithesis to that of Hawkins; and so in many respects it was. But that is by no means the whole story. Lester's style was in most important respects complementary to Hawkins's rather than antagonistic to it. Where the antithesis lay was with some of the white saxophonists who began to set the tone and ambience, whose playing went absolutely against the grain of all that men like Hawkins, Hodges, and Charlie Parker, had achieved and stood for, for big sound, the full-blooded approach to life and art. Some of these others, like Paul Desmond and Lee Konitz, and even at times Stan Getz, eschewed the forthright assumptions and often sounded like maiden ladies doing embroidery. But this could never be charged against Lester Young himself. That, as much as anything, and though it is still not fully recognized, was why Lester himself was out in the cold at the same time as Hawkins, displaced by his own disciples who had progressively diluted and devitalized the style he had created.

To hear how ridiculous it is to suggest that Coleman Hawkins and Lester Young could not share the same world and accept equal honours in it, one has only to listen to them playing together on the same bill. According to Norman Granz, this first happened at a Jazz at the Philharmonic concert on 22 April 1946. Whether this is strictly true or not is hardly relevant; what is relevant is that items from this concert are preserved on records and show how idiotic it is and always has been to set two supreme masters of the tenor saxophone against each other as though the fashion of the moment was in the least important or meaningful in time's cold eye.

It is unlikely that Coleman Hawkins played a major part, either by precept or example, in the evolution of the bop idiom of the 1940s, as some have suggested. What is more likely is that his alert and highly intelligent mind sensed changes coming, anticipated them in a number of ways, responded to them when they did come but without being a total part of them in the sense that their actual creators were. Also, now that the ruckus caused by the bop 'revolution' is more than thirty years distant, the dust laid, the casualties counted, we can see more clearly than anyone could at the time or near to it that bop demonstrably confirms Belá Bartók's argument that in art there are no revolutions, only slow or fast developments. In jazz the bop emergence was certainly, or appeared so at the time, a fairly fast development; but in retrospect it can be seen how many of its elements grew out of the preceeding age, but no less how the whole of jazz's evolution parellels that of European 'straight' music in a number of important respects. The shift from a predominantly diatonic music to a predominantly chromatic one, which was an important characteristic of the bop evolution, can be seen as a parallel with the post-Wagnerian move to extreme chromaticism and then beyond into atonality and seriality. The parallels may not be exact, few parallels are, but they are near enough for plotting the course on the chart.

For the moment, then, Hawkins continues on his magisterial way, recording, fulfilling club and concert engagements, using modernists or mainstream musicians as and when he pleased or as his convenience or inclination prompted. Although he frequently uses the harder tone and more driving approach he had been developing during the latter part of his stay in Europe, he can still show himself the supreme master of the romantic rhapsodic ballad style, which some continue to see as decadent, his tone beautifully rich and seductive, his style almost caressing, though at its best never cloying.

If Hawkins stands as one of the supreme giants of jazz, it is largely because of the great range and depth of his expressive powers. There have been many who might equal him in one or other aspect of the art, but few who equal the total gamut of ends and means. Perhaps only Louis Armstrong stands on a similar eminence; even Lester Young, though he excelled Hawkins in certain aspects of his work could not seriously rival Hawk's immense range.

To undertake a detailed review of all Hawkins's recording activities during these years would lead through labyrinthine ways, all leading towards much the same ends. It was valuable to do so in the case of his

7 Publicity still, 1940s (Melody Maker)

European years, partly because it helped to demonstrate the still developing course of his working career, partly because the recordings themselves pinpointed his physical presence in various places and countries. But after his return to the States the position was different. All the same, a few indicators and milestones need to be given. Hawk often recorded *On the Sunny Side of the Street* (who hasn't?), but the 1944 version with Tab Smith (as), Don Byas (ts) and Harry Carney in the front line produced something special from a session which also included a very fine *Make Believe*. Another first-rate session from 1944 produced, under the name of drummer Cozy Cole, four excellent tracks, including *Blue Moon* and *Just One More Chance* by a group that featured, besides Cole and Hawk himself, Earl Hines, Joe Thomas and Trummy Young. The 1945 Capital session, with a group that included trumpeter Howard McGhee and pianist Sir Charles Thompson, produced *Stuffy*, a track that has become something of a touchstone for what may be called mid-period Hawkins, Hawkins, that is, pitched between the dying swing era and the new bop style. This session also produced a new version of *It's the Talk of the Town*, a number which Hawk had made famous in his classic 1933 version with Fletcher Henderson. It has not quite the magic of its predecessor, but it still has huge style and confidence. There was also another *Stardust* and a very good *April in Paris* plus an equally good *Wrap Your Troubles in Dreams*. All in all, this was one of the best mid-1940s sessions for Hawkins.

In 1947 he made a couple of sessions with modernists Fats Navarro (t), J.J. Johnson (tb), Max Roach (d) and Milt Jackson (vib). This is perhaps the nearest Hawk ever came to total identification with the world of bop: it was largely but not totally successful. There is more than a hint that Hawkins's former absolute authority was beginning to be undermined, though the cracks are still only slight and by no means fatal. Yet in retrospect one can see the insidious onset of that period of unhappiness and neglect which Hawk was to go through from the end of the 1940s and well into the 1950s.

Partly because he was already beginning to feel the cooling wind of changing fashion, Hawk joined Norman Granz's Jazz at the Philharmonic not long after its inception. (Its first concert took place on 2 July 1944 at the Los Angeles Philharmonic Auditorium.) It was hardly the ideal setting for Hawkins. He never turned down a challenge, but Granz's policy of setting contrasting (and often incompatible) soloists against each other in a kind of Roman arena was not the sort of musical environment for a man of Hawk's sensitivity and musicality. If it did not always tempt him into vulgarity – and it was a setting especially suitable for musical vulgarians – it seldom sparked him to his very best. All the same, he still managed to create some excellent music in the JATP setting.

In 1949 Coleman Hawkins revisited Europe. He made an appearance in Paris at the *Semaine du Jazz* and then returned the following year for a tour under the auspices of the celebrated French critic Charles Delaunay who, with the other central figure on the Parisian jazz scene, Hugues Panassié, virtually founded the European style of jazz appreciation and criticism. Delaunay himself was the pioneer jazz discographer, his *Hot Discography* which first appeared in 1936 being the first serious attempt to bring the then chaotic jumble of jazz recordings into some sort of order. Unhappily, though, the 1940s were not the 1930s in jazz or any other terms, and Hawkins's return was hardly a triumphant progress through his old haunts. Public taste had changed and public memory was short, understandably in view of how the years of war that had torn the old Europe apart. Hawk's reception was cool and Delaunay's pocket damaged. It must have been a considerable disappointment to both and have increased Hawkins's sense of musical and stylistic isolation.

Though he worked and toured with JATP and continued to play dates and make records, Hawk was increasingly being made to feel the chill wind of capricious fashion. It was sometime about now that he is reported to have said with some bitterness that he would not want any children of his to go into the music business. It is scarcely surprising, then, that his playing around this time showed increasing moments of uncertainty, that he seemed to be living off his old mastery, which never quite deserted him, but without adding anything to it. That he could still pull something new and exciting out of the depository of his great talents is proved by some of the records he made. *Picasso*, which he recorded for Norman Granz in 1948, and is a quite remarkable example of that most difficult of undertakings, a completely unaccompanied solo. It is not perhaps the sort of thing one can live on and off indefinitely, but as a *tour de force* in answer to a particular challenge it showed that Coleman Hawkins could still play most of his rivals off the stand, whatever style they chose to adopt for the occasion.

All the same, the first half of the 1950s did find Hawk with somewhat – clipped wings. He made some more records, but they tended to be either poorly planned or against the natural grain. Some rather gushing effusions were mixed with some at the opposite pole suggesting a kind of frustrated anger expressed with coarse tone and rhythmic obstinancy. In both cases, the feeling cannot be avoided that Hawkins had come to the conclusion, fortunately a passing one, that it was all not really worth the effort.

Hawkins's huge talent enabled him to cross many frontiers of style and technique; but there were some things even he could not do and certainly did not want to do. One of these was to de-emotionalize, as it might be, his natural means of expression. For the moment the maiden ladies had taken over jazz, and they and their disciples were affronted by the big tone emotionalism of Coleman Hawkins and others of a similar persuasion. Of course the big men of the 'cool' school (call it what you will) never sneered or turned their backs. But big men do not command the fashionable world; that is populated by innumerable small fry whose particular pleasure comes from snapping at their betters who happen for the time being to have fallen out of favour. Fashions can often be valuable in breaking down too set and rigid assumptions and in letting fresh air into musty places, as well as opening doors to new ideas and fresh talents. The trouble is that fashion itself soon becomes rigid and inflexible, and like the noisiest revolutionaries, whether in art or politics, soon become not true conservatives but outright obstructionists. The jazz world has always been particularly susceptible to this, and as a consequence many real talents have been forced into the cold, sometimes forever.

It passed, as it always passes. A change swept through the jazz world, bringing back another kind of emotionally committed style, making the term 'hot jazz' no longer a dirty word, though now in another form and a different context. Something called 'hard bop' began to emerge and the tenor saxophonists who were associated with it returned to a more robust style and a more complete tonal resource. The dominant figures in this new development were John Coltrane and Sonny Rollins; but in fact this was the beginning of the domination of the jazz scene by the tenor saxophone, its practitioners proliferating in every corner.

The resurrection of Hawkins's morale and mastery appears to have taken place sometime during the later 1950s. At that time there was a revival of interest in the musicians of the swing period, and many who had been either forced into part-time musical activity or pushed out of music altogether began to find themselves in renewed demand. The

Prestige record label in particular began to record such musicians, and Coleman Hawkins was one to reap advantage. A succession of Prestige dates brought forth music worthy of the old master. But before dealing with these in some detail, it is perhaps best to take note of what may in retrospect be seen as the key session for Hawkins's newly revived authority and confidence – that arranged by the English critic and writer Stanley Dance as part of a series in which he did full honour to musicians who had suffered unjust neglect. Titled 'The High and Mighty Hawk' it was appropriately named, especially in the long track *Bird of Prey Blues* with its seventeen masterful choruses by Hawkins. One aspect of the Parker-led bop evolution had been the conception of the long solo as a unity in itself rather than as a succession of choruses. In *Bird of Prey Blues* Hawkins reconciled the two concepts; he built a totally unified and cohesive solo on the basis of what outwardly appeared as a succession of choruses in the old manner. It was a magnificent achievement by any standards, and in no sense a self-regarding exhibition such as Paul Gonsalves's marathon 27 choruses between Duke Ellington's *Diminuendo in Blue* and *Crescendo in Blue*, a piece of rabble-rousing vulgarity which destroyed one of Duke's finest compositions. The comparisons may not be fair, because Gonsalves was playing at the Newport Festival in 1956 while Hawkins was part of a serious jazz session in the studio, with no groundlings to scatter. All the same, it does indicate how the intellectual quality of Hawkins's best work raises it high above most of that of the average talented but more or less conventional soloists. The entire album as issued showed Hawk in his old majestic form, assisted by a fine group which included Buck Clayton, Hank Jones (p), Ray Brown (b) and Mickey Sheen (d). These memorable sessions took place on 18 and 19 February 1958.

The first of the Prestige sessions took place on 28 February 1958 and was entitled 'Blue Groove' by a group under the joint leadership of Hawkins and guitarist Tiny Grimes. It produced in *Marching Along* a classic Hawkins performance, plus yet another well proportioned *April in Paris*. The group, including pianist Ray Bryant, also contains some mildly inconsequential flute musings by Musa Kaleem, but the overall impression is one of robust and forthright jazz. The combination, minus flute, is one which Hawkins particularly favoured at this time. The next session, with Bryant again on piano, Kenny Burrell (g), Wendell Marshall (b) and Osie Johnson (d), took place on 7 November. It was issued as 'Soul' and was less successful than its predecessor, although the obeisance to the current fashion was more titular than real, and Hawk as usual goes mostly his own masterful way. 'Hawk Eyes', the next Prestige session, again has Tiny Grimes on guitar and this time the forceful Charlie Shavers on trumpet. This reinforces the claim that Coleman Hawkins and the new tenor players were on a parallel wavelength.

29 April 1959 brought a curious session which featured four tenors – Hawkins, Eddie 'Lockjaw' Davis, Buddy Tate and Arnett Cobb – with organist Shirley Scott and George Duvivier (b) and Arthur Edgehill (d). A number of jazz organists were coming through at this time, including Jimmy Smith, Jack McDuff and Jimmy McGriff, but Shirley Scott was always one of the most lyrical and imaginative. The session of 12 August was more interesting, in that it teamed Hawkins with the Red Garland Trio. Garland was a modernist pianist, talented but somewhat overrated at the time, who with Paul Chambers and Philly Joe Jones formed what came to be known as The Rhythm Section, and appeared with many leading front-line men of the time, including Miles Davis, Art Pepper and John Coltrane. The particular juxtaposition was intriguing, and showed another facet of Hawk's power and adaptability. Garland's heavily chordal style contrasted effectively with Hawk's power of swing and decisive manner of improvization, to produce music that was perhaps rather more embryonic than fully achieved, but still revealed latent possibilities. On numbers like *Red Beans*, *Bean's Blues* and *It's a Blue World* what emerges is on the whole more actual than potential.

The Coleman Hawkins All-Stars session on 8 January 1960 had Hawk with Joe Thomas (t), and Vic Dickenson (tb) sharing the front line, and supported by Tommy Flanagan (p), Wendell Marshall (b) and Osie Johnson (d). Again, it does not quite come together, Thomas in particular sounding as though he was at the time feeling his way rather than finding it; but Dickenson is in memorably unsentimental form. *You Blew Out the Light* and *Cool Blue* stand out.

Two further sessions, 'At Ease with Coleman Hawkins' (29 January 1960) and 'The Hawk Relaxes' (28 February 1961) reveal Hawkins in the kind of indolent mood he could so easily assume, excellent playing but perhaps just too much taking his mastery for granted. Another session in between, 'Night Hawk' made on 30 December 1960, has Hawkins teamed with Eddie 'Lockjaw' Davis plus a rhythm section of Tommy Flanagan, Ron Carter (b) and Gus Johnson (d). This is considerably more spirited and finds Hawk and 'Lockjaw' striking genuine sparks from each other.

Hawkins at this time was more and more inclined to play just with a rhythm section of piano, bass and drums, with sometimes a guitar added. He settled in the early 1960s with a more or less permanent quartet of himself, Flanagan, Major Holley (b) and Eddie Locke (d), and with this group he made some showtime albums for Prestige. This too was a popular habit of the period, Shelley Manne's jazz version of 'My Fair Lady' gaining particular acclaim and setting a pattern often emulated. A more robust and forthright example of the quartet's work, however, appeared not on Prestige but from ABC Paramount (originally issued in the UK by EMI) under the title 'Today and Now'. This shows Hawk in imperious mood, swinging robustly and rhapsodizing purpose-fully through *Go Li'l Liza, Swingin' Scotch*, Quincy Jones's *Quintessence*, and taking a sideways look at *Don't Sit Under the Apple Tree* and *Put on Your Old Grey Bonnet* with a certain sly relish. This was recorded on 9 September 1962. Just under a month earlier he had made another Prestige album with the same group, 'Make Someone Happy' (16 August), not strikingly memorable, and on 14 September the quartet was augmented by Kenny Burrell (g), and Ray Barretto (conga) to pick up the current fashion for Latin Americanisms, with an album under the joint names of Hawkins and Burrell and entitled 'Bluesy Burrell'.

Either side of 1960 Hawkins was unusually busy even for him in the recording studios. He did an intriguing set with Milt Jackson under the title of 'Bean Bags' on which the huge-toned Hawkins matched his playing most judiciously to the more refined tone of Jackson's vibraharp, backed by a rhythm team of Flanagan, Burrell, Eddie Jones (b) and Connie Kay (d). The inclusion of Connie Kay gives the music a kind of half Modern Jazz Quartet feel, with 'Bags' in his own particular musical orbit. There have been reports that Hawk made some disparaging remarks about the restrained, fragile sounding (at first hearing) music of MJQ; but there is not much sign of it here, despite some rather stereotyped critical reviews written at the time. Hawk obviously knew, what most of us have always known, that you do not have to make a great noise or fuss to swing, and that MJQ's real roots are deep in the mother-earth of jazz. Also around this time he did a couple of sessions with a group consisting of Thad Jones (t), Eddie Costa (p & vibes), George Duvivier (b) and Osie Johnson (d). These too have a curiously mixed feel. This is not to suggest that the music falls between

8 Benny Carter, Coleman Hawkins & Roy Eldridge, early 1960s
(Melody Maker)

stools or any commonplace judgment of that sort; simply that Jones, and to a less extent Costa, come from a different jazz background from Hawkins and that the results inevitably reflect it. In fact they find Hawk in ripe late form, showing yet again his strong musical insight, the range of his style and expression, and his ability to adapt to whatever company he may chance to find himself in. He was by no means always at his best as the 1960s progressed; but it was never safe to assume that he was not from any immediate appearances. It is, as always, necessary to listen, not to assume. Coleman Hawkins was always active but never entirely consistent: like all really big men, he cannot be categorized, cannot be taken at face value, cannot be relied on not to miss aim or take the wrong aim. Like all such, he perpetrated the imperfection of epics rather than the perfection of miniatures.

From the mid-1950s on Hawkins had begun to feature twelve-bar blues. Before that he had seldom resorted to the classic blues form, and when he did take to it he predictably came to it in his own way and from a personal angle. To say that Coleman Hawkins was one of the small handful of undisputed jazz masters and yet was not a great blues player may well seem an inadmissable paradox. It will certainly be seen in that light by conventional criticism, which tends to support the traditional view that great jazz playing is automatically to be equated with great blues playing. And if one thinks of most of the great jazzmen – Armstrong, Hodges, Parker, Nanton, Wells – they were all great blues men, masters of that central style out of which many would claim jazz is and always has been made at its best and most creative. Coleman Hawkins was not, in that sense, a great blues player. Yet it is no less true that his achievement was not only to bring the tenor saxophone as a major voice into jazz but, while so doing, to extend and expand the jazz language itself. If he was not a great blues player *per se*, his music was at all times infused from within with a feel of the blues, the inner spirit of the blues without their specific form and the physical delineation of the strict blues.

Yet that is still not a sufficient explanation. It is too easy to make vague references to blues feeling without going a step or two farther. Hawkins's assumption of the authentic blues manner and style comparatively late in his life suggests that it was not for him the most natural and immediate means of expression. On the other hand, many who proclaim themselves blues players (or singers) or style their bands in such terms, frequently have no more real connection with the blues than the regular interjection of the word into their vocabulary. Coleman Hawkins, although he did not adopt the form or use the word in the earlier part of his career, was one for whom the blues was a background rather than a springboard, a racial inheritance so ingrained that it did not need to be called into the foreground while his attention was musically engaged elsewhere.

Unlike a number of other tenor players, Hawkins was not a particularly good accompanist. Too often he tended to force his tone, to set up lines of contest with a singer or other instrumentalist. This is well exemplified on recordings by singers, notably Jimmy Rushing and Juanita Hall, in which he appears as part of an *ad hoc* accompanying group. He seldom sounds comfortable, and as a consequence the tracks on which he is prominent are seldom comfortable either. And this is a direct consequence of the way the blues is not his natural musical medium. He never seemed quite to understand or, if he did, to accept the understanding, that the blues is essentially a duet form. Big Bill Broonzy used to say that 'I make my guitar answer, but I don't never let it talk at the same time as me.' That is the voice of the true blues master. Hawkins never seemed to learn the lesson; he tended to 'talk' at the same time as the singer, to muscle in when he should either have been silent or confined to gentle commentary; and when he came forward to solo he often seemed to reveal an impatience that was alien to the idiom. It might be said that this was largely because he was such a dominating soloist that he found it difficult to subdue himself to a singer. But that does not really hold water. Louis Armstrong was nothing if not a dominating soloist; and yet Louis was a superb accompanist, right from the early days when as a very young man he often backed Bessie Smith. But Louis had learnt the lesson as second cornet to King Oliver back in the early 1920s, and he never forgot. He probably did not have to learn in the first place, because the blues idiom was as natural to him as his feeling for jazz improvization and he did not need formal lessons to remind him. But this was obviously not so for Coleman Hawkins. It does not make him a lesser musician, or in any way displace him from his place as one of the great jazzmen, one of the select handful. It simply sets him down as a different one.

It is well known that there are many jazzmen not of the undisputed first rank who are outstanding blues players. Among tenors Buddy Tate is certainly superior to Hawkins as a blues player, so is Lucky Thompson, though few would argue that either is a greater musician overall. On the Jimmy Rushing record in question, 'Little Jimmy and the Big Brass', Tate's contributions are much superior to Hawk's; but the real lesson in instrumental blues playing and accompanying comes, as so often, from Dicky Wells, another supreme exponent of that difficult art, at his finest on a level with Louis Armstrong. Hawkins, in this one department, never approached that standard, and perhaps never aspired to. His greatness lay elsewhere.

The brief review I have given of Hawk's records, as another bare chart of his career during the 1950s and into the 1960s, is not intended to be complete. (See for further and more detailed information the selected discography prepared by Tony Middleton at the end of this book.) But a few further additions are worth including. As a kind of spinoff of Hawkins's association with JATP came a 1958 set of more or less standard popular tunes made with the then Oscar Peterson Trio, plus drummer Alvin Stoller. It is not a demanding set, though it makes excellent listening as Hawk explores into a number of well-known melodies; but Oscar Peterson gives an object lesson in the art of the accompanist. Whatever one may think of his solo work, no one can question the superiority of Oscar's accompaniments.

During the later years Hawkins worked frequently with his old colleague from the Henderson days, Roy Eldridge. There were times when Roy's tendency to over-exuberance had provoked Hawk into answering in kind, not to his particular advantage. Yet at its best, the Hawkins/Eldridge partnership produced richly vital and genuinely exciting music. If the idea of Norman Granz's JATP was that of 'selling excitement' Hawk and Roy certainly promoted it. But both were better musicians than promotional vulgarities of that sort suggested. All the same, the habit did tend to persist, as on a 1965 effusion with Earl Hines under the title of 'Grand Reunion' which took place at the Village Vanguard and contains some noticeably undisciplined playing from both (though it also contains a rewarding *The Man I Love* from Roy alone). Hawk and Roy at their best struck genuine sparks out of each other, but the best of their collaborations seem never to have found a place in the record catalogues. They played often at the Metropole Café and, from contemporary reports, were frequently both exciting and creative. Much superior is a session that took place on 9 April 1959, when Roy Eldridge joined three leading tenor players, Hawkins, Ben Webster and Budd Johnson, plus a rhythm section of Jimmy Jones (p), Les Spann (g), Ray Brown (b) and Jo Jones (d). This contains four shortish pieces and one long one, a full LP side on Ellington's *In A Mellotone*, with a particularly striking solo by Johnson.

Hawkins and Webster appeared together on record more than once, and they usually made music worth remembering. The relationship between Hawkins and Webster throws up an interesting sidelight on the whole question of influence, and of the difficulty some younger men experience in escaping from the domination of an outstanding master. There is a story of how the young Ben Webster worked hard to get a good sound from his horn, and after he had worked for some time, his friends said to him, in effect: 'That's right, Ben; now you've got it. Now you sound just like Hawkins.' It was intended as a compliment, but Ben did not seen it that way. He wanted to be the first Ben Webster not the second Coleman Hawkins, so he went off and worked some more, and in the end he evolved a genuinely personal style based partly on the rich instrumental resources of Hawkins, partly on the resplendent lyricism of Johnny Hodges, retaining the tonal richness of Hawkins in the body of the instrument but adding a floating quality inherent in Hodges's alto sound. It is a salutary lesson that needed learning by a lot more people than actually learned it, and not only in respect of the tenor saxophone.

During his last years Hawk seemed gradually to be losing his interest in both life and music. More and more he sounded as though he was playing from memory; the fire was slowly sinking and although it could be fanned into brief burst of the old flame, the former power and glory had substantially departed. His last recording of all, made on 20 December 1966 for Norman Granz's Pablo label and entitled 'Sirius', reveals a man at the end of his tether though not yet quite played out and certainly not defeated. Over all of the nine tracks hangs an inescapable sense of spiritual and technical valediction. Because of it some of the playing is almost unbearably moving, not in the old passionate way of at times almost frightening authority, but that sense one often has in the last works of old men of a crumbling ruin that yet retains some aura of majesty and departing beauty. To look for the high and mighty Hawk through these tracks is to miss the point and to court disappointment. But to accept them in the spirit in which they were offered is to add a further mite to the understanding of a great and magnificent, if now slowly failing, man of jazz.

Coleman Hawkins died on 19 May 1969. His end was infinitely sad. He simply lost interest – in particular he lost interest in food, and without food all men must die. It sounds simple, even bizarre, set down plainly like that. But in fact it indicates a whole lot more than it says, a whole lot more than appears on or near the surface. It is difficult to escape the conclusion that the bitterness and disillusion that temporarily claimed him during the early 1950s never again quite left him. It sank into the deeper recesses of his psyche and consciousness, and even if he did seem to recover much of his old power and authority, there is evidence in his later playing, not least in its tendency to near ungovernable aggressiveness upon occasion, that the ire had entered his soul and had lodged there permanently. However that may be, he left this world, if not with a whimper, certainly not with a bang. He did, at the end, go gentle into that good night.

Out of Nowhere

The last time I saw Coleman Hawkins, in the late 1960s, he had come to London with the Oscar Peterson Trio and was appearing at the Queen Elizabeth Hall. He was already ill and had only a year or two still to live, but although he looked frail and grizzled, even unkempt by his own standards, he seemed to be in tolerably good nick. He laughed and talked in the bar beforehand and responded with a lively riposte when Oscar, no doubt remembering Hawk's familiar tight-fistedness, quipped that he still had not cashed in his last cheque from Fletcher Henderson. On stage he looked even more frail. Holding a horn that all at once seemed several sizes too big for him and rocking gently on the balls of his feet, he looked out at the audience with a slightly bemused smile, and acknowledged the generous applause as though he was not quite sure if it really was for him. Gone was the dapper Hawk of the old days; whatever confidence he may have felt inside did not show. But the moment he started to play, all was changed, changed utterly, and if the beauty that was then born was not exactly terrible, it was deeply moving. Suddenly the hall was filled with the great organ tones of his tenor saxophone. That is no exaggeration: the sound was immense and immensely resonant, recalling the former days and glories. The vibrations could be felt through the entire auditorium, just as they are when the organ sounds. The transformation was immediate and remarkable. And so it was the other way. The moment he finished playing, there he was, a little frail old man again. I have said that Oscar Peterson is a superb accompanist, and so he is. All the same, he was never Hawkins's favourite; Hawk liked a simple, more direct style behind him. He tended to find Oscar's approach too fussy. He preferred Tommy Flanagan. It worked, but there was a slightly jarring note.

Sometimes, it is true, there was more the echo of old mastery than the mastery itself. It was hardly surprising that the bird of prey's flight was not quite as imperious as once it had been, that both the spirit and the flesh were fallible. How should they not be? He had served and honoured his art and his profession for all but fifty years. The life of a jazz musician is never an easy one, even for the most favoured and talented of its practitioners. Jazzmen live hard and work hard, as they have to if they are to prevail in the jungle of the entertainment business. And more than most they are at the mercy of the whims of fashion and the indifferent shifts of taste and predilection, not least among those who might have been thought their most loyal friends and supporters. It takes a tough

71

9 Hawkins in the early 1960s (John Hopkins)

man to survive that kind of life into active old age. Coleman Hawkins was tough, but even he was not quite indestructible.

It is not entirely right to say that Coleman Hawkins came out of nowhere, although it is an argument that could be sustained in his case more than most. The other instrumentalists had some form of technical background to start from, some broad general guidelines. The brass players and the clarinettists had the military bands and the broader ranges of the symphony orchestra; the pianists had the whole long tradition of keyboard development as well as the more adjacent ragtime to call upon. But saxophonists had little but a small influence from French miliary bands, almost certainly unknown to them, and a very small injection from a few modern symphonic works which featured the saxophone. And the tenor saxophone had received virtually no attention or development of its scope and nature.

Perhaps the first technical question therefore is where did Hawkins's huge tone and tonal control come from? Benny Green was right when he said that the sound produced by Coleman Hawkins was not at all what Adolfe Sax originally had in mind. Sax was thinking of a thinner, more reedy sound. But this would not do for the jazzmen. They, at least some of them, like Hawkins, Bechet, Hodges, Carney, wanted a richer, more passionate sound. And they achieved it by a process that can only be understood in the light of the instrument's specific nature and structure.

Sax's invention appeared around 1840. It is in fact a hybrid among wind instruments. It is made of brass, conical in bore, and played with a single reed. It shares its single reed and 'stopped pipe' structure with the clarinet, but its conical bore with the oboe. Yet the oboe is played with a double reed. The single or beating reed attached to the conical brass tube was certainly an original idea in the fertile mind of its inventor; but though ingenious, it does have a number of musical disadvantages. Major problems of tuning tend to arise mostly with the soprano version, but the actual tonal structure of the sound is a potential limitation in all members of the family.

The main tonal limitation is that all saxophones tend to be strong in the fundamental but comparatively weak in harmonics. Thus the 'straight' or natural tone has a somewhat thin and nasal quality which is effective for some purposes but monotonous over long stretches. This is no doubt what Sax wanted, but it would not do in the long run. In order therefore to increase the saxophone's scope the basic tone had to be strengthened; steps needed to be taken to bring the relationship between

73

the fundamental and the harmonic structure into a more satisfactory balance. And this was done by increasing the wind pressure, not to produce, necessarily, a louder sound but to alter the tonal structure, by a species of judicious and controlled overblowing, something which on brass instruments produces coarse and 'splayed' tone but on the saxophone produces tonal richness. It also has the effect of forcing the sound deeper into the body of the instrument where the relationship between the fundamental and the harmonics tends to be freed from the domination of the former.

The white saxophone players, like Jimmy Dorsey and Frankie Trumbauer, who played a curious weapon called the C-melody saxophone, a hybrid within a hybrid pitched between alto and tenor, and who greatly influenced Lester Young, tended to favour a 'purer', more 'straight' sound; and later, when the 'cool' school emerged the full, rich passionate tone of the Bechet/Hodges/Hawkins manner was frowned upon. These later players, such as Lee Konitz and Paul Desmond, favoured a style based on a sound produced more in the neck of the instrument than in the bell, and thus seemed to reverse the major jazz priorities – until, that is, one recognises all jazz sounds are produced by a greater or less modification of conventional techniques and tone production.

Thus the Hawkins 'big sound' was the product of a deliberate attempt to alter the basic tonal structure of his instrument. And in the context it was necessary. All styles of musical performance, in whatever area, are closely linked to tonal resource and individual sound. As with all major performers, Coleman Hawkins's sound is an essential part of his overall style and manner. It is as closely related to what he did and how he played as his harmonic and rhythmic sense. His classic *Body and Soul* could not have been played as it was with a different sound. The essence of that famous performance, as indeed of all Hawkins's best rhapsodic work, lies in a fusion of several different elements, of which the tonal blend and balance is one of the most significant. Hawkins's way with a ballad, from *One hour* to his last examples forty years later was upon the quite simple principle of taking the basic musical skeleton of the tune and fleshing it out with harmonic tissue and relevant ornament. The title *Body and Soul* is oddly apt. The body of the tune is the skeleton, the harmonic and ornamental matter the soul. It is when, as sometimes happened with Hawkins and frequently with less gifted people who address themselves to this difficult art of rhapsodizing, the skeleton gets lost in a mush of ornament and harmonic irrelevance that the perform-ance falls apart from lack of internal cross bracing, and then what comes out appears as 'formless'.

Coleman Hawkins's harmonic sense was always highly developed. But it was fundamentally a diatonic sense, a telling and judicious use of chromatics, at bottom the exception rather than the rule. At least to begin with. As jazz developed and itself became more chromatic, so did Hawk's style. He never went as far in that direction as Lester Young, let alone Charlie Parker, whose exceptional harmonic audacities took him into far regions hardly dreamt of in jazz before. Although Hawkins's harmonic insights enabled him to come to immediate terms with the bop evolutions, it never caused a rupturing of his own deeply personal style, as it did a number of others who lost their way in the process. 'Keeping up with the times' can be a dangerous and futile process if not backed by considerable strength of character. Mutton dressed as lamb is as depressing and as undignified in music as in sartorial fashions.

How well apparent incompatibles may go together can be seen in the one studio recording Hawkins made with Parker, *Ballade*, cut in October 1950. Here Hawk's magisterial statement has something of what Henry James called 'the equanimity of a result' while Bird's succeeding har-monic excavations reveal what lay behind Hawkins's act of faith. Another interesting juxtaposition is the treatment of the old English tune *Greensleeves*, first by Hawkins and then by John Coltrane. These par-ticular recordings were made some years apart, yet the comparative relevance remains. Hawkins, as might be expected, treats the tune to one of his powerfully rhapsodic treatments, romantic but not sentimental (the tune was originally a New Year carol, not a lovesick dirge), while Coltrane operates on it with the scalpel of the soprano saxophone. Indeed, the juxtaposition goes farther than that. It also has a tonal relevance. Hawkins's later tone, harder and more aggressive, had a considerable influence on the so-called 'hard bop' school of tenorists, Coltrane and Sonny Rollins in the van. After his neglect during the 'cool' period, Hawkins returned to favour and influence. The tough tone of the hard boppers was clearly Hawkins-derived. Coltrane's tone, which often sounded as though it had been hollowed out on an anvil, relates directly to some of Hawkins's more truculent effusions; and Hawk's way of interjecting cascades of demisemiquavers into his solos, which threatened at one time to become a mannerism, can now be seen as a kind of parallel to Coltrane's 'sheets of sound'.

10 Coleman Hawkins, late 1960s (Hans Harzheim)

Coleman Hawkins spent his whole life playing the tenor saxophone. He left little time for anything else. He believed that the jazz musician should be at least as technically proficient as his classical counterpart, that the player of the tenor saxophone should have the same command of his instrument as Casals had of his cello. And like Casals, he believed that however long he lived and however much he played, there was always something still to learn. As a man he was quiet and reticent; he kept his private life private. He was married, but he always kept his wife behind the scenes, never involved her in the rough and tumble of a professional musician's working life. His one eccentricity seems to have been that he always liked to keep a Cadillac parked outside his house. He was not, from all reports, a very good driver, and he did not use the car to go to his work in New York. But it apparently reassured him to have it parked where he could see it, in front of his dwelling. How many he wrecked or allowed to deteriorate, we do not know, apart from the one he burnt out in 1934 chasing the Henderson band from Kansas City to St Louis after the shootout with Lester Young and the other KC roughnecks. Even men of apparently equable temperament, like Hawkins, must be permitted their private quirks, even though this one does not seem quite to tally with his notorious tightness with money.

'The Duke Ellington of the tenor saxophone', Paul Gonsalves called him; and Nat Hentoff once referred to him as 'the Victor Hugo of the tenor saxophone.' Obviously, to have been the actual Coleman Hawkins of the tenor saxophone must have been quite something. A classic for sure, one of the half dozen or so outstanding jazz soloists.

The poet Gerard Manley Hopkins wrote of Felix Randall, the farrier, as 'big boned and hardy-handsome'. I think that fits, as well as anything, the musical personality of Coleman Hawkins.

A Selective Discography

I have based my selections on titles referred to in the text and records generally available at the time of going to press. Further listening suggestions follow the main discography. The following abbreviations have been used: (arr) arrangement;(as) alto sax; (b) bass; (bars) baritone sax; (bj) banjo; (cl) clarinet; (cor) cornet; (d) drums; (f) flute; (g) guitar; (p) piano; (tb) trombone; (tp) trumpet; (ts) tenor sax; (tu) tuba; (vcl) vocal; all other instruments given in full. Locations: LA (Los Angeles); NYC (New York City). Only records issued in: (Eu) Europe and (Am) United States of America are noted. If a record is only currently available in (J) Japan, this too is included.

TONY MIDDLETON *London,* August 1984

McKINNEY'S COTTON PICKERS
Joe Smith, Leonard Davis, Sidney de Paris (tp); Claude Jones (tb); Don Redman (as, cl, vcl); Coleman Hawkins, Ted McCord (ts); 'Fats' Waller (p, celeste); Dave Wilborn (bj); Billy Taylor (tu); Kaiser Marshall (d).   *NYC. November 5, 1929*

57064-2	PLAIN DIRT	RCA (Eu) PM42407
57065-1	GEE, AIN'T I GOOD TO YOU	"

as November 5, 1929   *NYC. November 6, 1929*

57066-2	I'D LOVE IT	RCA (Eu) PM42407
57067-1	THE WAY I FEEL TODAY	"
57068-2	MISS HANNAH	"

Note: other titles on PM42407 do not include Coleman Hawkins.

as November 5, 1929   *NYC. November 7, 1929*

57139-3	PEGGY	RCA (Eu) PM43258
57140-2	WHEREVER THERE'S A WILL THERE'S A WAY (My baby)	"
57140-3	WHEREVER THERE'S A WILL THERE'S A WAY (My baby)	"

Note: other titles on PM43258 do not include Coleman Hawkins.

MOUND CITY BLUE BLOWERS
Red McKenzie (comb); Glenn Miller (tb); Pee Wee Russell (cl); Coleman Hawkins (ts); Eddie Condon (bj); Jack Bland (g); Al Morgan (b); Gene Krupa (d).
NYC. November 14, 1929

57145-3	HELLO, LOLA	RCA (Eu) FXM1 7325
57146-3	ONE HOUR	"

Note: For other titles refer October 11, 1939 and January 3, 1940.

FLETCHER HENDERSON AND HIS ORCHESTRA
Russell Smith, Rex Stewart, Bobby Stark (tp); Jimmy Harrison, Claude Jones (tb); Benny Carter (as, cl); Harvey Boone (as); Coleman Hawkins (ts); Fletcher Henderson (p); Clarence Holiday (g); John Kirby (b); Walter Johnson (d).
NYC. October 3, 1930

W150857-1	CHINATOWN, MY CHINATOWN	CBS (Eu) 66423
W150858-3	SOMEBODY LOVES ME	"

Note: for other Henderson titles referred to in the text see sessions September 1933 and June 1934. See also 'further listening suggestions' following main discography.

MOUND CITY BLUE BLOWERS
Red McKenzie (comb, vcl); Muggsy Spanier (cor); Jimmy Dorsey (as, cl); Coleman Hawkins (ts); Jack Russin (p); Eddie Condon (bj); Jack Bland (g); Al Morgan (b); Josh Billings (d).   *NYC. June 30, 1931*

404966-C	GEORGIA ON MY MIND	CBS (Eu) 68227
404967-B	I CAN'T BELIEVE THAT YOU'RE IN LOVE WITH ME	"
404994-A	THE DARK TOWN STRUTTERS BALL	"
404995-A	YOU RASCAL YOU	"

Note: 68227 is a double LP with most of Hawkins recordings for Columbia 1930–1941

80

SPIKE HUGHES AND HIS ALL AMERICAN ORCHESTRA

Shad Collins, Leonard Davis, Bill Dillard (tp); Dicky Wells, Wilbur de Paris, George Washington (tb); Benny Carter (as, cl, vcl); Wayman Carver (as, cl, fl); Howard Johnson (as, cl); Coleman Hawkins (ts, cl); Red Rodriguez (p); Lawrence Lucie (g); Ernest Hill (b); Kaiser Marshall –1, Sid Catlett –2 (d); Spike Hughes (arr).

NYC. April 18, 1933

B13257-A	NOCTURNE –1	Jasmine (Eu) JASM2012
B13258-A	SOMEBODY STOLE GABRIEL'S HORN vBC, –1	"
B13259-A	PASTORALE –2	"
B13260-A	BUGLE CALL RAG –2	"

same as April 18, 1933 except Red Allen (tp), Luis Russell (p) replace Shad Collins and Red Rodriguez. Add Chu Berry (ts) omit Kaiser Marshall.

NYC. May 18, 1933

B13352-A	ARABESQUE –3	Jasmine (Eu) JASM2012
B13353-A	FANFARE	"
B13354-A	SWEET SORROW BLUES	"
B13355-A	MUSIC AT MIDNIGHT	"

Note: –3 omit piano

Red Allen (tp, vcl); Dicky Wells (tb); Benny Carter (as); Wayman Carver (fl); Coleman Hawkins, Chu Berry (ts); Red Rodriguez (p); Lawrence Lucie (g); Spike Hughes (b); Sid Catlett (d). *NYC. May 18, 1933*

B13356-A	SWEET SUE	Jasmine (Eu) JASM2012

same as big band May 18, 1933 except that Benny Carter also plays soprano sax. *NYC. May 19, 1933*

B13359-A	AIR IN D FLAT	Jasmine (Eu) JASM2012
B13360-A	DONEGAL CRADLE SONG	"
B13361-A	FIREBIRD	"
B13362-A	MUSIC AT SUNRISE	"

same as small band May 18,1933. *NYC. May 19, 1933*

B13363-A	HOW COME YOU DO ME LIKE YOU DO? vRA	Jasmine (Eu) JASM2012

FLETCHER HENDERSON AND HIS ORCHESTRA

Russell Smith, Bobby Stark, Red Allen (tp); Claude Jones, Dicky Wells (tb); Hilton Jefferson, Russell Procope (as); Coleman Hawkins (ts); Horace Henderson (p); Bernard Addison (g); John Kirby (b); Walter Johnson (d).

NYC. September 22, 1933

W265135-2	QUEER NOTIONS	World Records (Eu) SHB42
W265136-3	IT'S THE TALK OF THE TOWN	"
W265137-2	NIGHT LIFE	"
W265138-2	NAGASAKI –1	"

Note: –1 Red Allen, vocal.

COLEMAN HAWKINS AND HIS ORCHESTRA

Red Allen (tp); J. C. Higginbotham (tb); Hilton Jefferson (as, cl); Coleman Hawkins (ts); Horace Henderson (p); Bernard Addison (g); John Kirby (b); Walter Johnson or Sid Catlett (d). *NYC. September 29, 1933*

W265143-2	THE DAY YOU CAME ALONG	World Records (Eu) SHB42
W265144-2	JAMAICA SHOUT	"
W265145-2	HEARTBREAK BLUES	"

HORACE HENDERSON AND HIS ORCHESTRA
same as Fletcher Henderson session September 22, 1933.

		NYC. October 3, 1933
W265150-2	HAPPY FEET	World Records (Eu) SHB42
W265151-1	RHYTHM CRAZY	,,
W265152-1	OL' MAN RIVER –1	,,
W265153-2	MINNIE THE MOOCHER'S WEDDING DAY	,,
W265154-1	AIN'T 'CHA GLAD	,,
W265155-1	I'VE GOT TO SING A TORCH SONG	,,

FLETCHER HENDERSON AND HIS ORCHESTRA
same as October 3, 1933 except Joe Thomas (tp), Keg Johnson (tb), Vic Engle (d) replace Bobby Stark, Dicky Wells and Walter Johnson. Add Buster Bailey (cl) and Charles Holland (vcl). *NYC. March 6, 1934*

BS81787-1	HOCUS POCUS	RCA (Eu) PM43691
BS81788-2	PHANTOM FANTASIE	,,
BS81789-2	HARLEM MADNESS vCH	,,
BS81790-1	TIDAL WAVE	,,

Note: other titles on PM 43691 are by Coleman Hawkins with Fletcher Henderson's orchestra 1927 and 1931.

COLEMAN HAWKINS (ts)
accompanied by Buck Washington (p). *NYC. March 8, 1934*

W265172-2	IT SENDS ME	World Records (Eu) SHB42
W265173-2	I AIN'T GOT NOBODY	,,
W265175-1	ON THE SUNNY SIDE OF THE STREET	,,

COLEMAN HAWKINS (ts)
accompanied by Stanley Black (p); Albert Harris (g); Tiny Winters (b)

		London. November 18, 1934
CE6739-1	LULLABY	World Records (Eu) SHB42
CE6740-1	LADY BE GOOD	,,
CE6741-1	LOST IN A FOG –1	,,
CE6742-1	HONEYSUCKLE ROSE –1	,,

Note: –1 omit guitar and bass. SHB42 also contains two recordings by Coleman Hawkins with Jack Hylton's Orchestra, 1939. Remaining titles are by other artists.

COLEMAN HAWKINS QUARTET
Coleman Hawkins (ts); Freddy Johnson (p); Fritz Reinders (g); Jacques Pet (b); Kees Kranenburg (d). *Laren, Holland. April 27, 1937*

AM381-1	SOMETHING IS GONNA GIVE ME AWAY	Jasmine (Eu) JASM2011

Note: other titles on JASM2011 are 1935/1937 recordings in Holland with The Ramblers. For details of other recordings in Europe during this period refer to 'further listening suggestions' following main discography.

COLEMAN HAWKINS AND HIS ALL STAR JAM BAND

Benny Carter (tp, as, arr); André Ekyan (as); Alix Combelle (ts, cl); Coleman Hawkins (ts); Stephane Grappelly (p); Django Reinhart (g); Eugene D'Hellemmes (b); Tommy Benford (d).   *Paris, France. April 28, 1937*

OLA1742-1	HONEYSUCKLE ROSE	World Records (Eu) SM643
OLA1743-1	CRAZY RHYTHM	"
OLA1744-1	OUT OF NOWHERE	"
OLA1745-1	SWEET GEORGIA BROWN	"

COLEMAN HAWKINS AND HIS ORCHESTRA

Tommy Lindsay, Joe Guy (tp); Earl Hardy (tb); Jackie Fields, Eustis Moore (as); Coleman Hawkins (ts); Gene Rodgers (p); William Oscar Smith (b); Arthur Herbert (d); Thelma Carpenter (vcl).   *NYC. October 11, 1939*

042933-8	MEET DOCTOR FOO	RCA (Eu) FXM1 7325
042934-12	FINE DINNER	"
042935-2	SHE'S FUNNY THAT WAY	"
042936-1	BODY AND SOUL	"

Note: for other titles refer November 14, 1929 and January 3, 1940.

COLEMAN HAWKINS ALL STAR OCTET

Benny Carter (tp); J. C. Higginbotham (tb); Danny Polo (cl); Coleman Hawkins (ts); Gene Rodgers (p); Lawrence Lucie (g); Johnny Williams (b); Walter Johnson (d).
                                                 NYC. January 3, 1940

046156-1	WHEN DAY IS DONE	RCA (Eu) FXM1 7325
046157-1	THE SHEIK OF ARABY	"
046158-1	MY BLUE HEAVEN	"
046159-1	BOUNCING WITH BEAN	"

Note: for other titles refer November 14, 1929 and October 11, 1939. FXM1 7325 also includes a 1940 Jam Session plus three radio broadcast titles by Hawkins' Orchestra from the Savoy Ballroom in July and August 1940.

COLEMAN HAWKINS AND THE CHOCOLATE DANDIES

Roy Eldridge (tp); Benny Carter (as); Coleman Hawkins (ts); Bernard Addison (g); John Kirby (b); Sid Catlett (d).   *NYC. May 25, 1940*

A2995-1	SMACK	Commodore (Eu) 6.24056
A2995-4	SMACK	"
A2996-1	I SURRENDER DEAR –1	"
A2996-	I SURRENDER DEAR –1	"
A2997-1	I CAN'T BELIEVE THAT YOU'RE IN LOVE WITH ME	"
A2997-	I CAN'T BELIEVE THAT YOU'RE IN LOVE WITH ME	"
A2998-1	DEDICATION –2	"

Note: –1 Benny Carter plays piano, –2 omit trumpet and alto. Other titles refer December 4, 1943

COLEMAN HAWKINS AND LEONARD FEATHER'S ALL STARS

Cootie Williams (tp); Edmond Hall (cl); Coleman Hawkins (ts); Art Tatum (p); Al
Casey (g); Oscar Pettiford (b); Sid Catlett (d).   *NYC. December 4, 1943*

A4691-1	ESQUIRE BOUNCE	Commodore (Eu) 6.240566
A4691-2	ESQUIRE BOUNCE	,,
A4692-1	BOFF BOFF (Mop mop)	,,
A4692-2	BOFF BOFF (Mop mop	,,
A4693-1	MY IDEAL	,,
A4693-2	MY IDEAL	,,
A4694-1	ESQUIRE BLUES	,,
A4694-2	ESQUIRE BLUES	,,

Note: other titles refer May 25, 1940.

COLEMAN HAWKINS AND HIS ORCHESTRA

Bill Coleman (tp); Andy Fitzgerald (cl); Coleman Hawkins (ts); Ellis Larkins (p); Al
Casey (g); Oscar Pettiford (b); Shelly Manne (d).   *NYC. December 8, 1943*

T1905	VOODTE	Doctor Jazz (Eu) ASLP1004
T1906	HOW DEEP IS THE OCEAN	,,
T1907	HAWKINS' BARREL HOUSE	,,
T1908	STUMPY	,,

COLEMAN HAWKINS QUARTET

Coleman Hawkins (ts); Eddie Heywood (p); Oscar Pettiford (b); Shelly Manne (d).
NYC. December 23, 1943

T1923	CRAZY RHYTHM	Doctor Jazz (Eu) ASLP1004
T1924	GET HAPPY	,,
T19005	THE MAN I LOVE	,,
T19006	SWEET LORRAINE	,,

Note: other titles on ASLP1004 are by Lester Young.

COLEMAN HAWKINS'S ALL AMERICAN FOUR

Coleman Hawkins (ts); Teddy Wilson (p); John Kirby (b); Sid Catlett (d).
NYC. May 29, 1944

HL33	MAKE BELIEVE	Mercury (J) BT5254
HL34	DON'T BLAME ME	
HL35	JUST ONE OF THOSE THINGS	,,
HL36	HALLELUJAH	,,

Note: other titles on BT5254 are Keynote sessions by Hawkins from around this
period.

COLEMAN HAWKINS WITH WALTER THOMAS'S ORCHESTRA

Jonah Jones (tp); Eddie Barefield (as, cl); Hilton Jefferson (as); Coleman Hawkins,
Walter Thomas (ts); Clyde Hart (p); Milt Hinton (b); Cozy Cole (d).
NYC. October 11, 1944

IN THE HUSH OF THE NIGHT/OUT TO LUNCH/LOOK OUT JACK!/EVERY MAN FOR
HIMSELF   Harlequin (Eu) HQ2004

COLEMAN HAWKINS QUARTET

Coleman Hawkins (ts); Thelonius Monk (p); Edward Robinson (b); Denzil Best (d).
NYC. October 19, 1944

DRIFTING ON A REED/RECOLLECTIONS/FLYIN' HAWK/ON THE BEAM
                                    Harlequin (Eu) HQ2004

Note: other titles on HQ2004 are by Ben Webster.

COLEMAN HAWKINS AND HIS ORCHESTRA
Howard McGhee (tp); Coleman Hawkins (ts); Sir Charles Thompson (p); Allan Reuss (g); Oscar Pettiford (b); Denzil Best (d).   *LA. February 23, 1945*

573	APRIL IN PARIS	Music for pleasure (Eu) 2MO56-80802
574	RIFFTIDE	"
575	STARDUST	"
576	STUFFY	"

same as February 23, 1945 except Howard McGhee on first title only and Vic Dickenson (tb) added for first and second titles only.   *LA. March 2, 1945*

585	HOLLYWOOD STAMPEDE	Music for pleasure (Eu) 2MO56-80802
586	I'M THROUGH WITH LOVE	"
587	WHAT IS THERE TO SAY	"
588	WRAP YOUR TROUBLES IN DREAMS	"

Note: most other discographical works have not noted the above personnel changes. McGhee was unwell after recording HOLLYWOOD STAMPEDE and Vic Dickenson left the studio after recording the first two titles.

same as February 23, 1945 except John Simmonds (b) replaces Oscar Pettiford.
LA. March 9, 1945

593	TOO MUCH OF A GOOD THING	Music for pleasure (Eu) 2MO56-80802
594	BEAN SOUP	"
595	SOMEONE TO WATCH OVER ME	"
596	IT'S THE TALK OF THE TOWN	"

COLEMAN HAWKINS
unaccompanied tenor sax solo.   *1948*
PICASSO   Verve (Eu) 2304537
Note: other titles on 2304537 are selections of Coleman Hawkins recordings for Verve 1948–1958

COLEMAN HAWKINS QUARTET
Coleman Hawkins (ts); Hank Jones (p); Ray Brown (b); Buddy Rich (d).
NYC. September 18, 1949
BODY AND SOUL/RIFFTIDE/SOPHISTICATED LADY   Verve (Eu) VRV3

COLEMAN HAWKINS QUARTET
same as September 18, 1949   *NYC. September 16, 1950*
YESTERDAYS/HAWK'S TUNE/STUFFY   Verve (Eu) VRV3
Note: the above titles are from a JATP concert at Carnegie Hall. See September 18, 1949 for other titles. Also refer to October 19, 1957.

ALLEN/HAWKINS
Red Allen (tp); J. C. Higginbotham (tb); Sol Yaged (cl); Coleman Hawkins (ts); Lou Stein (p); Milt Hinton (b); Cozy Cole (d).   *NYC. 1957*
BATTLE HYMN OF THE REPUBLIC/BLUES/WON'T YOU COME HOME BILL BAILEY/ SOUTH/WHEN THE SAINTS GO MARCHING IN   Jazz Groove (Eu) 002
Note: other titles refer August 7, 1958.

COLEMAN HAWKINS ALL STARS
Idrees Sulieman (tp); J. J. Johnson (tb); Coleman Hawkins (ts); Hank Jones (p); Barry Gailbraith (g); Oscar Pettiford (b); Jo Jones (d).   *NYC. March 12 & 15, 1957*
CHANT/JUICY FRUIT/THINK DEEP/LAURA/BLUE LIGHTS/SANCTICITY
Riverside (Am) OJC 027

COLEMAN HAWKINS' NEWPORT ALL STARS

Roy Eldridge (tp); Pete Brown (as); Coleman Hawkins (ts); Ray Bryant (p); Al McKibbon (b); Jo Jones (d). *Rhode Island. July 5, 1957*

MOONGLOW/I CAN'T BELIEVE THAT YOU'RE IN LOVE WITH ME/SWEET GEORGIA BROWN –1 Verve (Eu) 2304369

Note: –1 Roy Eldridge (d) replaces Jo Jones. Coleman Hawkins does not perform on other titles, all from Newport Jazz Festival.

HAWKINS-ELDRIDGE

Roy Eldridge (tp); Coleman Hawkins (ts); John Lewis (p); Percy Heath (b); Connie Kay (d). *Chicago. October 19, 1957*

BEAN STALKIN'–1/TEA FOR TWO/THE WALKER–1/KERRY/I CAN'T GET STARTED–1/TIME ON MY HANDS –1/BLUE MOON/COCKTAILS FOR TWO Verve (Eu) 2304432

Note: –1 mono versions of these titles are on Verve (Eu) VRV3

COLEMAN HAWKINS ALL STARS

Buck Clayton (tp); Coleman Hawkins (ts); Hank Jones (p); Ray Brown (b); Micky Sheen (d) *NYC. February 18/19, 1958*

GET SET/BIRD OF PREY BLUES/MY ONE AND ONLY LOVE/VIGNETTE/OOH-WE MISS G.P./ YOU'VE CHANGED Master Jazz Records (Am) MJR8115

HAWKINS-ALLEN

Red Allen (tp); Earl Warren (cl); Coleman Hawkins (ts); Marty Napoleon (p); Chubby Jackson (b); George Wettling (d). *NYC. August 7, 1958*

MEAN TO ME/STORMY WEATHER/LONESOME ROAD/SLEEPYTIME GAL/SUMMERTIME/ ALL OF ME/TEA FOR TWO Jazz Groove (Eu) 002

Note: for other titles refer 1957.

COLEMAN HAWKINS QUINTET

Coleman Hawkins (ts); Ray Bryant (p); Kenny Burrell (g); Wendell Marshall (b); Osie Johnson (d). *NYC. November 7, 1958*

1641	I HADN'T ANYONE TILL YOU	Prestige (Eu) OJC 096
1642	GREENSLEEVES	"
1643	GROOVIN'	"
1644	SUNDAY MORNIN'	"
1645	UNTIL THE REAL THING COMES ALONG	"
1646	SWEETNIN'	"
1647	SOUL BLUES	"

COLEMAN HAWKINS SEXTET

Charlie Shavers (tp); Coleman Hawkins (ts); Ray Bryant (p); Tiny Grimes (g); George Duvivier (b); Osie Johnson (d). *NYC. April 3, 1959*

1744	STEALIN' THE BEAN	Prestige (Eu) HBS6115
1745	THROUGH FOR THE NIGHT	"
1746	LA ROSITA	"
1747	HAWK EYES	"
1748	C'MON IN	"
1749	I NEVER KNEW	"

COLEMAN HAWKINS QUARTET
Coleman Hawkins (ts); Eddie Higgins (p); Bob Cranshaw (b); Walter Perkins (d).
Chicago. August 9, 1959
ALL THE THINGS YOU ARE/CENTERPIECE/BODY AND SOUL/JUST YOU JUST ME
Spotlite (Eu) SPJ137

Note: other titles refer June 12, 1963.

HAWKINS-POWELL
Coleman Hawkins (ts); Bud Powell (p); Oscar Pettiford (b); Kenny Clarke (d).
Essen, Germany. April 2, 1960
YESTERDAYS/ALL THE THINGS YOU ARE/STUFFY/JUST YOU JUST ME
Black Lion (Eu) BLP30125

Note: other titles do not include Coleman Hawkins.

COLEMAN HAWKINS QUARTET
Coleman Hawkins (ts); Tommy Flanagan (p); Major Holly (b); Eddie Locke (d).
NYC. August 13, 1962
ALL THE THINGS YOU ARE/JOSHUA FIT THE BATTLE OF JERICHO/MACK THE KNIFE/IT'S
THE TALK OF THE TOWN   Verve (J) 23MJ3295
Note: recorded at the Village Gate club.

COLEMAN HAWKINS QUARTET
Coleman Hawkins (ts); Tommy Flanagan (p); Major Holly (b); Eddie Locke (d).
NYC. September 9, 1962
GO LI'L LIZA/QUINTESSENCE/DON'T LOVE ME/LOVE SONG FROM APACHE
Jasmine (Eu) JAS38

same as September 9, 1962.   *NYC. September 11, 1962*
PUT ON YOUR OLD GREY BONNET/SWINGIN SCOTCH/DON'T SIT UNDER THE APPLE
TREE   Jasmine (Eu) JAS38

same as September 11, 1962 plus Barry Gailbraith, Howard Collins (g); Willie
Rodriguez (percussion); Manny Albam (arr).   *NYC. September 12, 1962*
SAMBA ARA BEAN/I'M LOOKING OVER A FOUR LEAF CLOVER/SAMBA DE OMA NOTA SO/I
REMEMBER YOU   Jasmine (Eu) JAS12

same as September 12, 1962   *NYC. September 17, 1962*
DESAFINADO/UM ABRACO NO BONFA/O PATO/STUMPY BOSSA NOVA
Jasmine (Eu) JAS12

same as September 9, 1962.   *Chicago. June 12, 1963*
THE WAY YOU LOOK TONIGHT/I CAN'T GET STARTED/MOONGLOW
Spotlite (Eu) SPJ137
Note: recorded at the London House club. Other titles refer August 9, 1959.

COLEMAN HAWKINS ORCHESTRA
Bill Berry (tp); Urbie Green (tb); Coleman Hawkins (ts); Barry Harris (p); Buddy
Catlett (b); Eddie Locke (d).   *NYC. February 22, 1965*
WRAPPED TIGHT/INTERMEZZO/MARCHETA   Jasmine (Eu) JAS50

Snooky Young (tp) replaces Bill Berry.
RED ROSES FOR A BLUE LADY/SHE'S FIT/BEAUTIFUL GIRL/OUT OF NOWHERE –1/INDIAN
SUMMER –1   Jasmine (Eu) JAS50
Note: –1 omit tp and tb.

same as February 22, 1965.   *NYC. March 1, 1965*
BEAN'S PLACE/AND I STILL LOVE YOU   Jasmine (Eu) JAS50

COLEMAN HAWKINS with Earl Hines Trio
Coleman Hawkins (ts); Earl Hines (p); George Tucker (b); Oliver Jackson (d).
                                                              NYC. March 1965
CRAZY RHYTHM/ROSETTA/JUST ONE MORE CHANCE/RIFFTIDE/INDIAN SUMMER
                                                              Pumpkin (Am) 105

COLEMAN HAWKINS QUARTET
Coleman Hawkins (ts); Barry Harris (p); Bob Cranshaw (b); Eddie Locke (d).
                                                              NYC. December 20, 1966
THE MAN I LOVE/DON'T BLAME ME/JUST A GIGOLO/THE ONE I LOVE BELONGS TO
SOMEBODY ELSE/TIME ON MY HANDS/SWEET AND LOVELY/EXACTLY LIKE YOU/
STREET OF DREAMS/SUGAR   Pablo (Eu) 2310707

Further listening suggestions

THE FLETCHER HENDERSON STORY 'A study in frustration'. 64 titles recorded between 1923 and 1938 in which the Coleman Hawkins period with Henderson is well documented. This four LP box set also contains an informative 20 page booklet. CBS (Eu) 66423.

RAMBLING AROUND. 1935 recordings in Holland with The Ramblers. PANACHORD (Eu) H2006.
MADE IN HOLLAND, 1934–1937. PANACHORD (Eu) H2005.
MADE IN HOLLAND, 1937–1938. Duo and trio recordings in Holland. PANACHORD (Eu) H200

IN CONCERT. 1944/1946 radio broadcast and concert performances featuring Roy Eldridge and Billie Holiday. PHOENIX (am) LP8

COLEMAN HAWKINS AND THE TRUMPET KINGS. Various 1944 small group recordings for Keynote with Roy Eldridge, Buck Clayton and Charlie Shavers. MERCURY (Eu) 6336325.

BEAN-A-RE-BOP. Four titles May 1944 with Charlie Shavers, six originally recorded for Asch January 11, 1945 and four Aladdin sides from June 1947 with Miles Davis. QUEEN DISC (Eu) Q 038.

COLEMAN HAWKINS/LESTER YOUNG. February–April 1945 radio broadcasts including the 'Hollywood Stampede' group. SPOTLITE (Eu) SPJ 119.

DISORDER AT THE BORDER. September 1952 radio broadcasts from the Birdland club NYC, with Roy Eldridge, Horace Silver, Art Blakey and others. Also includes an interview with Hawkins. SPOTLITE (Eu) SPJ 121.

FAVORITES. Fifties small group radio broadcasts and concert performances. SHOESTRING (Am) SS 107.

THE HAWK TALKS. 1952–1953 Decca recordings mainly with orchestral accompanyments. JASMINE (Eu) JASM 1031.

COLEMAN HAWKINS MEETS THE SAX SECTION. Hawkins with members of the 1958 Count Basie saxophone and rhythm sections. SAVOY (Am) SJL 1123.

TENOR GIANTS. A double LP containing two great Hawkins LP recordings. Coleman Hawkins meets Ben Webster 1957 and Coleman Hawkins with Webster, Bud Johnson and Roy Eldridge 1959. VERVE (Eu) 2610046.

CENTERPIECE. September 19, 1959 small group date plus September 1, 1962 radio broadcast. PHOENIX (Am) LP 13.

BENNY CARTER AND HIS ORCHESTRA 'Further definitions'. Carter, Hawkins, Phil Woods, Charlie Rouse plus rhythm section in November 1961 recreations similar to the Paris session in April 1937. JASMINE (Eu) JAS 14.

DUKE ELLINGTON MEETS COLEMAN HAWKINS. 1962 recording of Hawkins with an Ellington small group including Nance, Brown, Hodges etc. JASMINE (Eu) JAS 1.

COLEMAN HAWKINS AT NEWPORT JAZZ FESTIVAL with Lambert, Hendricks and Bevan. RCA (Eu) PL43531, and with Joe Williams RCA (Eu) NL70119. July 1963.

SONNY MEETS HAWK! July 1963 recording Coleman Hawkins with Sonny Rollins Quartet, part of Sonny Rollins double LP RCA (Eu) 741074/5.

FLETCHER HENDERSON ALL STARS. 1957 reunion directed by Rex Stewart. MUSIDISC (Eu) JA5210.

REX STEWART/COOTIE WILLIAMS. MUSIDISC (Eu) JA5201.

DUKE ELLINGTON and BUCK CLAYTON ALL STARS AT NEWPORT. Coleman Hawkins is featured in the Clayton titles in this July 1956 recording. CBS (Eu) 88605.

Note: the following suggestions have not been available for some time but a knowledgeable jazz shop may help you locate them.

1958 date for Atlantic with Milt Jackson.

Double LP of Hawkins reminiscing (verbally), recorded in 1956 and issued on Riverside (Eu) RLP 12–117/118.

Big band recordings for RCA January 1956.

CAPITOL recordings 1956/7 with large concert orchestra.

Many fine LPs for Prestige/Swingville/Moodsville 1958–1962.

The following are also noted in the text.

CHARLIE PARKER QUINTET
Charlie Parker (as); Coleman Hawkins (ts); Hank Jones (p); Ray Brown (b); Buddy Rich (d). *NYC. October 1950*
BALLADE   Verve (Eu) 817445.1
Note: other titles do not include Coleman Hawkins.

JOHN COLTRANE ORCHESTRA
Booker Little (tp); Britt Woodman (tb); Carl Bowman (euphonium); Julius Watkins, Don Corrado, Bob Northern, Bob Swisshel (french horns); Bob Barber (tu); Eric Dolphy (as, fl, bass clarinet); John Coltrane (ts, sop.); Laurdine Patrick (bars); McCoy Tyner (p); Reggie Workman, Art Davis (b); Elvin Jones (d).   *NYC. June 7, 1961*
GREENSLEEVES   Jasmine (Eu) JAS8
Note: LP title AFRICA BRASS.

Titles of LPs

PM42407 *The Complete McKinney's Cotton Pickers Vol 1 & 2* (1928–1929).

PM43258 *The Complete McKinney's Cotton Pickers Vol 3 & 4* (1929–1930).

FXM1 7325 *The Complete Coleman Hawkins Vol 1* (1929–1940).

JASM2012 *Spike Hughes and his All American Orchestra.*

SHB42 *Ridin' in rhythm.*

PM43691 *The Indispensable Fletcher Henderson* (1927–1936).

6.24056 *Commodore Classics.* (Am) XFL 14936.

ASLP 1004 *Classic tenors.*

HQ2004 *Bean and Ben.*

2MO56–80802 *Hollywood stampede.*

VRV3 *The Coleman Hawkins set.*

Jazz Groove 002 *Stormy weather.*

OJC 027 *The Hawk flies high.*

2304537 *All Stars at Newport.*

2304432 *At the Opera House.*

OJC 096 *Coleman Hawkins with Ray Bryant and Kenny Burrell.*

HB6115 *Hawk eyes!*

SPJ137 *Blowin' up a breeze.*

BLP30125 *Hawk in German*

23MJ3295 *Hawkins! Alive! At the Village Gate.*

JAS38 *Today and now.*

JAS12 *Desafinado.*

JAS50 *Wrapped tight.*

Pumpkin 105 *Coleman Hawkins with Earl Hines trio.*

2310707 *Sirius.*

Bibliography

For so important a musician, the Coleman Hawkins bibliography is extremely meagre. Perhaps his private temperament and largely taciturn nature were one reason. As it is, there was the small but expert book by Albert J. MacCarthy which appears in the Cassell 'Kings of Jazz' series in 1963, and the 'Solography – the Tenor Saxophone of Coleman Hawkins, 1929–1942' by Jan Evensmo, a promient Norwegian authority, the second and revised edition of which appeared in 1976.

In addition, there have been important articles on Hawk by Michael James in the old *Jazz Monthly* and by Max Jones in *Melody Maker*, both written while Hawkins was still alive and active. The contents of the double album of Hawk reminiscing (Riverside – see Discography) were once transcribed and printed in a small American magazine, but that has long disappeared. There are many references in books and many expert record reviews over the years; but the above is about the extent of major writings on Coleman Hawkins.